DARTS
MASTER

DARTS MASTER

THE OFFICIAL

QUIZ BOOK

David Clayton

First published by Pitch Publishing, 2025

1

Pitch Publishing
9 Donnington Park,
85 Birdham Road,
Chichester, West Sussex,
PO20 7AJ
www.pitchpublishing.co.uk
info@pitchpublishing.co.uk

© 2025, David Clayton

Every effort has been made to trace the copyright.
Any oversight will be rectified in future editions at the
earliest opportunity by the publisher.

All rights reserved. No part of this book may be reproduced,
sold or utilised in any form or transmitted in any form or by
any means, electronic or mechanical, including photocopying,
recording or by any information storage and retrieval system,
without prior permission in writing from the publisher.

A CIP catalogue record is available for this book
from the British Library.

ISBN 978 1 83680 218 1

Typesetting and origination by Pitch Publishing

Printed and bound in the UK on FSC® certified paper in line
with our continuing commitment to ethical business practices,
sustainability and the environment.

Printed and bound by CPI Group (UK) Ltd, Croydon, CR0 4YY

Contents

Acknowledgements 9

About the Quiz Compiler 10

Introduction 11

Questions 13

Answers. 121

For my mate and fellow Manchester City fan Alan 'Chuck' Norris. Looking forward to watching you climb the PDC world rankings again and hopefully playing a small part! Also, for my youngest daughter, Chrissie, for being my darts buddy and watching endless reruns of *Bullseye* on YouTube.

Acknowledgements

Thank you to Jane Camillin at Pitch Publishing for the opportunity to write this book. I've done a lot of books for Pitch over the years, and they are one of the best out there. As always, thanks to my family for their support as this took a heck of a lot of research and cross-checking to get 1,000 questions. Every effort has been made not to repeat any questions, but a couple might appear in different guises! The questions are all from reliable and official sources and were accurate as of 1 June 2025.

About the Quiz Compiler

David Clayton is a journalist for a leading English football club and the author of many sports books and biographies. He is married to Sarah and the father of Harry, Jaime and Chrissie. He has followed darts since his mum captained the local pub team and watched *Bullseye* religiously as a kid and never misses a PDC tournament on TV.

Ally Pally at Christmas is on his bucket list!

Introduction

How much do you really know about darts? You can discover the depth of your knowledge by exploring the 1,000 questions set in the 100 categories that make up this darts treasure trove.

Discover the identity of the man known as 'The Voice of Darts', learn which multi-World Champion was given the unwanted nickname of 'The Crafty Potter' and which martial arts legend led to Alan Norris's nickname.

All of the above, plus facts and questions on Luke 'The Nuke' Littler, and even the players who scored biggest on the cult TV show *Bullseye*.

You will be entertained for hours and learn so much more about the game that is bigger than ever before, both in the UK and around the world. The ultimate companion to one of the most loved sports in Britain!

Quiz 1

The Easing-You-In Points Quiz

What better way to start off a 1,000 question quiz book than with questions you probably know the answers to?

This is all about scores, slang, and terms ...

1. What is the maximum score any dart player can achieve with three throws?
2. How much is a double top worth?
3. How many points is a bullseye worth?
4. What area of the board is worth 25 points per throw?
5. What treble is known as 'The Devil'?
6. Which two numbers are either side of 20?
7. What is a single, double and treble of the same number known as?
    a. Singapore Sling
    b. Shanghai
    c. Tokyo Treble.
8. What is a 'Bag of Nuts' a darts slang for?
9. What is the diameter of the bullseye?
    a. 10.7mm
    b. 12.7mm
    c. 14.7mm.
10. What does each player need to begin scoring at the PDC World Grand Prix?

Quiz 2

Scores on the Doors Quiz.

Here are some more scoring conundrums for you to solve ...

1. What is the lowest score you can achieve if three darts all score?
2. What is the highest scoring single, double and treble worth of the same number?
3. What are three bullseyes worth?
4. True or false – if you hit three bullseyes in one throw, you have won the game?
5. How many points are three outer bullseyes worth?
6. What is the lowest score possible with three trebles?
7. What is the highest score possible if you don't score a maximum of 180?
8. Is it possible to score zero with three darts?
9. What is the only way to score zero if your darts do hit the scoring part of the board?
10. How much is the highest treble other than 20 worth?

Quiz 3

Legends Quiz: Adrian Lewis.

Let's see how much you know about the man they call ... oh, wait, that's question 10!

1. How many PDC World Championships has Lewis won?
2. True or false – Lewis is from the same town as Phil Taylor?
3. Which year did he win the PDC UK Open?
4. Which former World Champion managed Lewis?
    a. Keith Deller
    b. John Lowe.
5. Who did Lewis partner at the 2012 World Cup of Darts?
6. Which Cockney pop star did Lewis once record a song with?
7. True or false – Lewis and Phil Taylor support rival teams?
8. In 2006, Lewis competed in his first PDC World Championship. How far did he get?
9. Who did he beat to win the 2011 World Championship final?
10. What is Lewis's nickname?

Quiz 4

The 'It's all Random' Quiz – Part 1.

An eclectic collection of darts trivia for you to solve ...

1. Who said, "My Gran told me the English poison the water"?
2. By what score did Luke Littler beat Michael van Gerwen in the 2025 World Championship final?
3. Who was the BDO Women's World Champion eight times out of the first ten finals?
4. Which nation did 1979 World Cup singles champion Nicky Virachkul represent?
5. Which betting company sponsored the 2025 World Championship final?
6. Which comedy horror movie sees the lead character pull a dart out of his head?
    a. Shaun of the Dead
    b. Hot Fuzz.
7. True or false – Charlie Chucker is a genuine professional darts player?
8. What was the total prize fund at the 2025 World Championship?
    a. £2m
    b. £2.5m.
9. How much did Luke Littler win at the above event?
10. Christian Kist and Damon Heta both achieved what at the 2025 World Championship?

Quiz 5

The Numbers and Colours Quiz.

Note: if you're colourblind, you may need a little help with this one ...

1. What colour is the bullseye bed on a dartboard?
2. What colour is the outer bullseye ring?
3. What colour is a Manchester Dartboard?
4. What colours are the trebles on a dartboard?
5. What colours are the doubles on a dartboard?
6. Typically, what colours will the referee and scoring officials wear at a PDC event?
7. What is the diameter of a typical dartboard?
8. What height should the centre of a dartboard be from the floor?
    a. Five feet 8 inches
    b. Six feet.
9. How far is the oche from the dartboard according to PDC rules?
    a. Seven feet
    b. Seven feet 5½ inches
    c. Seven feet 9¼ inches.
10. How many possible ways can a nine-darter be achieved?
    a. 3,944
    b. 4,022
    c. 4,202

Quiz 6

The We Are Premier League Quiz!

The PDC Premier League – how much do you know? Let's find out!

1. HAs of 2025, how many players compete in the PDC's Premier League?
2. Of the 13 seasons he competed in; how many Premier League titles did Phil Taylor win?
3. What do Sky Sports call the achievement of winning the World Championship, World Matchplay and Premier League?
4. How many Premier League games did Phil Taylor remain unbeaten for?
    a. 38
    b. 44
    c. 9.
5. From 2013 to 2023, how many times did Michael van Gerwen win the Premier League?
    a. Five
    b. Six
    c. Seven.
6. From 2022 to 2025, what was the total prize fund?
    a. £1m
    b. £1.5m
    c. £2m.
7. True or false – Gary Anderson is the only Scot to win the PDC Premier League?
8. Where were the Play-Offs held in 2025?
9. How many nine-dart finishes were there in the 2025 tournament?
10. As of 2025, who had more nine-dart finishes in the Premier League – Luke Littler or Luke Humphries?

Quiz 7

Legends of the Game Quiz.

This is all about the 'big dogs' and their sizeable achievements over the years – let's get into it ...

1. When did Phil Taylor win his first PDC World Championship title?
2. Who was the first ever PDC World Champion?
3. Who is the only North American to win the PDC World Championship?
4. How many PDC World Championship titles did Phil Taylor win?
5. How many years were there between Phil Taylor's first and last PDC World Championship titles?
6. How many PDC World Championship titles has Michael van Gerwen won?
7. How many titles have Dutch players won since 1995?
8. Who is the only Welshman to have won the PDC World Championship?
9. What have Adrian Lewis, Phil Taylor and Gary Anderson all got in common?
10. What was unique about the 2024 and 2025 PDC World Champions?

Quiz 8

The Nicknames Quiz – Part 1.

Nicknames and darts go together like strawberries and cream – or maybe beer and nuts – there's gonna be plenty of these quizzes so let's get going ...

1. Who is better known as 'Snakebite'?
2. Who is 'The Nuke'?
3. Which player is nicknamed 'Chuck'?
4. Who is known as 'The Flying Scotsman'?
5. Who is better known as 'Cool Hand'?
6. Which player goes by the name of 'Mighty Mike'?
7. Who is known as 'The Ferret'?
8. Who is 'The Iceman'?
9. Name the player better known as 'The Asp'?
10. Who is also known as 'The Bullet'?

Quiz 9

The PDC World Matchplay Quiz (as of June 2025).

One of the PDC's premier events, let's test your knowledge on the World Matchplay ...

1. Which year did the World Matchplay start?
2. What has been the venue every year, bar one?
3. What venue temporarily hosted the World Matchplay?
4. Which year was that?
5. Who did Larry Butler beat in the first World Matchplay final?
6. What nationality is Butler?
7. True or false – the 1995 World Matchplay was Jocky Wilson's last televised event?
8. With five losses as of 2025, who has been runner-up the most in the tournament?
9. Who has won more World Matchplay titles?
    a. Rod Harrington
    b. Rob Cross.
10. How many titles have been won by English players?
    a. 10
    b. 16
    c. 24.

Quiz 10

The Know Your Clockface Quiz.

We all know what a regulation dartboard looks like, don't we? Don't we ... ? We'll soon know the answer to that question which, for the record, isn't a question in this quiz. Best get on ...

1. Which two numbers would represent three o'clock on a dartboard?
2. Which two numbers sit either side of three?
3. True or false – 16 and eight are beside each other on a board?
4. Which two numbers sit either side of 18?
5. If you add the bottom three numbers on a board together, how much do you get?
6. Who makes the official PDC dartboard?
7. An easy one, which two numbers sit either side of 20?
8. If you scored double top, a devil and a bullseye in one shot, what is your score?
9. Can you name the numbers that sit either side of 14 on a board?
10. If you scored doubles across the top three numbers, what would your score be?

Quiz 11

Legends Quiz: James Wade.

One of the PDC's most consistent performers, let's test your knowledge on the Wademeister ...

1. As of 2025 how many World Championship semi-finals had Wade reached?
2. How many UK Open titles has Wade won as of 2025?
3. In 2010, Wade reached his highest world ranking – what was that?
4. Is Wade right or left-handed?
5. As of 1 June 2025, Wade had suffered a record of how many nine-dart finishes against him?
    a. 9
    b. 11
    c. 13.
6. Which former *Soccer AM* presenter did Wade date between 2008 and 2010?
7. In 2012, Wade was part of a charity single entitled 'Got My Tickets For the Darts' with who?
    a. Chas Hodges
    b. Bradley Walsh.
8. True or false – Wade suffers from bipolar disorder and ADHD?
9. Which venue has Wade says he prefers?
    a. Alexandra Palace
    b. Winter Gardens.
10. In which county was Wade born?
    a. Surrey
    b. Kent.

Quiz 12

Oh, Referee! The Russ Bray Quiz.

How much do you know about darts' legendary referee, Russ Bray? The great man has recently retired, but there are many strings to his bow, as you'll discover below ... Let's find out!

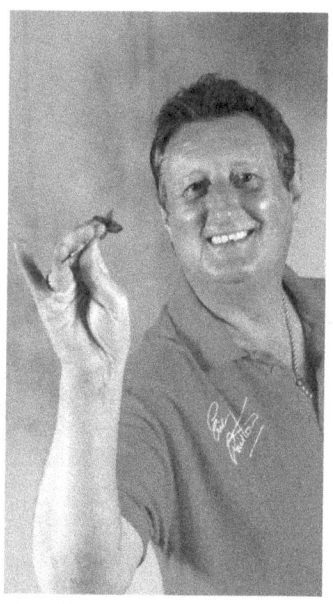
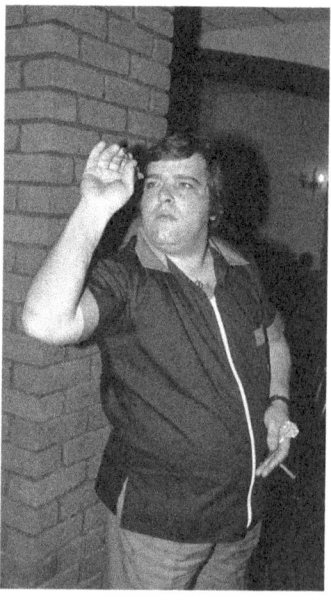

Question number 5.

1. How many years did Bray referee PDC tournaments for?
    a. 28 years
    b. 30 years
    c. 32 years.
2. What was his nickname?
3. True or false – Bray is a former traffic warden?
4. Which darts legend was Bray officiating when he threw his first televised nine-darter?
    a. John Part
    b. Phil Taylor.

5. Who did Bray team up with to win the Norway and Finland pairs?
    a. Eric Bristow
    b. Jocky Wilson.
6. Which *Guinness* World Record did Bray achieve on Blackpool's North Pier?
    a. Fastest recorded 180
    b. Hitting the bullseye from ten feet
    c. Eating a stick of rock in nine seconds.
7. Who competed in Bray's last televised final?
8. What role did Bray take on after retiring in 2024?
    a. PDC Ambassador
    b. Referee coach.
9. Which football team does Bray follow?
    a. Chelsea
    b. Tottenham
    c. West Ham.
10. Which other sport has Bray's voice been heard on, as an MC?
    a. Boxing
    b. Wrestling.

Quiz 13

The Darts General Trivia Quiz.

A bit of this and a bit of that ...

1. Which year was darts finally recognised as a sport by *Sport England*?
     a. 1995
     b. 2000
     c. 2005.
2. True or false – dartboards were once made of clay?
3. What weight must a dart not exceed?
4. Who said, "I wanted to find something, and I got it in the outfits and the crazy hair. I think the players who whinge about me are jealous."
5. In 2014, which TV show did legend John Lowe appear in?
     a. Amazing Greys
     b. Arrows & Sparrows.
6. The 2024 PDC World Championship final between Luke Littler and Luke Humphries was watched by a record TV audience – was it:
     a. 3.9m
     b. 4.8m.
7. True or false – most dartboards are made in India?
8. Who designs Peter Wright's hair?
     a. A local hairdresser
     b. He does it himself
     c. His Wife.
9. How many segments does a standard dartboard have?
     a. 78
     b. 82
     c. 86.
10. Which football club was PDC President Barry Hearn chairman of up until 2014?

Quiz 14

Legends Quiz: Michael van Gerwen.

One of the PDC's most imposing and popular figures, let's find out a bit more on MVG ...

1. As of 2025, how many times has MVG been World Champion?
2. How many Premier League titles had MVG won as of 2025?
3. What sport did MVG play regularly up to the age of 12?
4. True or false – MVG is also known as the '*Orange Giant*'?
5. What was MVGs job before turning professional?
    a. Tiler
    b. Mechanic.
6. What was the documentary by *Sky Sports* on MVG called?
    a. Magic Mike
    b. Mighty Mike.
7. True or false – MVG was knocked out of his first two PDC World Championships by Phil Taylor?
8. Which football team does MVG follow?
    a. PSV
    b. Ajax.
9. As of June 2025, how many televised nine-dart finishes had MVG achieved?
10. Is this statement true – MVG was World No.1 from 2014 to 2021?

Quiz 15

The Bristow or Mason Quiz.

Two of darts' most outspoken characters – Eric Bristow and Chris Mason – but which one said these quotes? There are five from Eric, five from Chris...

1. "I have two bowls of confidence for breakfast each morning."
2. "I do have spells where I get everything I want and then I just go missing. I can't put my finger on what I'm doing different when I do go missing."
3. "I'd hoped I'd go up there and play with a bit of freedom," he laughs. "I obviously retired a long time ago, but I came back because I wanted to support this more than anything. I didn't do this for me. But when I did start practising I thought, 'I can still do this.'"
4. "All this cuddling and kissing on stage these days, well it's all right in football when someone scores a goal, but not when you're playing darts."
5. "I would like to publicly apologise to Phil Taylor for my post-match outburst. I make no excuses for my behaviour and the words I chose to use."
6. "Even when I go on holiday I have a practice. It's in my blood."
7. "If the game you love doing all of a sudden you can't do any more, then you have to think, 'hang on a minute, I might not be able to do exhibitions here'. So what do you do at the age of 30 or whatever? Become a postman?"
8. "No, I wouldn't swap my life with how it is now," he tells *Daily Star Sport*. "I couldn't compete anyway. The levels have gone through the roof. It's about staying in your lane. I'm more about talking about it than playing in it. I prefer it that way."
9. "I like a drink, mate. I'll have maybe 10 or 12 pints on a good night out."

Chris Mason

10. "But without a doubt, I'm relishing the opportunity of playing in the Super Series and the Seniors. Whatever I do, I'll be giving it my all, but with a slightly different attitude. It's not as important, but once you've been competitive, you'll always be competitive. I will be trying my socks off."

Quiz 16
The Darts Pioneers Quiz – Part 1.

The Indoor League was one of the first TV shows to feature darts – but how much do you know about a show that really helped put darts on the map ...

1. How many years was *The Indoor League* on TV?
    a. 1971-1975
    b. 1972-1976
    c. 1973-1977.
2. Which cricket legend presented the show?
3. True or false – darts commentator legend Sid Waddell created the show?

Sid Waddell

4. Aside from darts, name three other games that were featured on the show?
5. How did the presenter sign off each show?
    a. By saving, "Ah'll see thee."
    b. By saying, "You'll be reet."
    c. By saying, "Take it easy."
6. In series one, what type of dartboard was used in games?
    a. Manchester board
    b. Doubles board
    c. Traditional board.
7. True or false – a doubles dartboard contains no trebles?
8. How many episodes were filmed in total?
    a. 62
    b. 65
    c. 68.
9. From which series did women compete in the darts competitions?
    a. The first series
    b. The second series.
10. Who won the inaugural Indoor League Darts Championship?
    a. Colin Minton
    b. Leighton Rees.

Quiz 17

The One and Only – It's the Sid Waddell Quiz.

The man who arguably did more for darts than any other as the sport began to grow into more than just a pub pastime. Let's see if you can figure out who the great Sid Waddell was talking about here ...

1. "His idea of exercise is sitting in a room with the windows open taking the lid off something cool and fizzy."
2. "He's not just an underdog, he's an underpuppy!"
3. "He has the consistency of a planet – and he's in a darts' orbit!"
4. "Once upon a time he was breaking all records, now he's only breaking his hearts. Nothing you can do, total eclipse of the dart."
5. "He comes from the valleys and he's chuffing like a choo-choo train!"
6. "When Alexander of Macedonia was 33, he cried salt tears because there were no more worlds to conquer. (name) is only 27!"
7. "He's not Adonis, he's THE Donis!"
8. "If we'd had (name) at Hastings against the Normans, they'd have gone home."
9. "He is striding out like Alexander the Great conquering the Persians."
10. "He went to see a psychologist and was told if he wants to get psyched up he should listen to Oasis. I reckon darts fans will get a Tungsten Supernova."

Quiz 18

Who's Favourite Doubles Quiz.

Darts players always have their favourite finish they work towards – that reliable double they have hit so many times ... so how many of the below can you figure out? It's a tough one, this! Can you name the doubles favoured by these ten players?

1. Mensur Suljović – what does he like to finish on whenever possible?
2. Gerwyn Price loves which double?
3. Rob Cross and Dimitri Van den Bergh like this double?
4. Which double does Stephen go Bunting mental for?
5. James Wade will always finish in this double's bed if he can?
6. Ryan Searle is sweet on this double?
7. Michael Smith scores roughly 50% of his double finishes with this number?
8. Does Jonny Clayton have a higher percentage success with double 16 or double 8?
9. Luke Littler is near-perfect on this number... what is it? – double 10 or double 20?
10. Dave Chisnall prefers this double?

Quiz 19

It's the Darts Cricket Quiz.

How much do you know about this worldwide darts game? Cricket is played in many countries and is one of the most popular of all alternative games on a dartboard – if you've not partaken, this might be tough – but what a way to learn!

1. True or false – Cricket is the most popular darts format in the USA?
2. What is darts cricket also known as in the UK?
3. How do you close a number in cricket?
4. Name another way you can close a number out?
5. Yes or no – the bullseye is required to win a game of cricket?
6. Traditionally, how do you choose who goes first in a game of cricket?
7. True or false – the TV show *Bullseye* was based on the game of cricket?
8. How many bullseyes do you need to hit in order to win a game of cricket?
9. Is it most often played on a soft tip electronic board or a steel tip board?
10. True or false – the real sport of cricket once tried to sue several darts governing bodies over the use of the name cricket?

Quiz 20

The Walk-on Music Quiz – Part 1.

This is one everyone has some knowledge of and is a favourite staple of any darts quiz – so why would we do any different? After a player has been introduced, these are the tunes that they hope will get the crowd going – but who do they belong to ... ?

1. 'Kölsche Jung' by Brings – who walks on to that?
2. Which Kiss classic does Dylan Slevin walk on to?
3. 'This Girl' by Kungs vs. Cookin' on Three Burners is who's walk-on music?
4. 'The Best' by Tina Turner is the walk-on music of whom?
5. Nick Kenny used a Britpop classic as his theme. Was it 'Song 2' by Blur or 'Wonderwall' by Oasis?
6. Jeffrey de Graaf – what is his walk-on music?
7. 'Jumping All Over the World' by Scooter – who walks out to that?
8. 'Hit Me with Your Best Shot' by Pat Benatar is the theme for who?
9. Keane Barry loves to rock the house with which AC/DC classic?
10. Connor Scutt's walk-on sounds like a greeting from Tarzan! What is it?

Quiz 21

The Know Your History Quiz.

Time to see how far your knowledge stretches back – if it's from Luke Littler's first World Championship final onwards, you may struggle!

1. When was the first recorded game of darts played in a pub?
    a. 1888
    b. 1908
    c. 1918.

2. The earliest known darts were believed to have been the stubs of what?
3. What did the first purpose-made darts use for flights?
4. What were the earliest darts made from?
    a. Metal
    b. Plastic
    c. Wood.

5. Though darts originated in Britain, which nation was credited with making the earliest darts to play with?
    a. The Netherlands
    b. Belgium
    c. France.
6. What did the 1990s Quadro Board uniquely have?
7. Which of these is not a darts game?
    a. Killer
    b. Cricket
    c. Tennis.
8. How does a Round the Clock game start?
9. What is the first number in the Round the Clock sequence?
    a. 20
    b. Bullseye
    c. 1.
10. When was the British Darts Organisation (BDO) founded?
    a. 1973
    b. 1975
    c. 1977.

Quiz 22

The This and That Quiz.

A bit of everything in here – trivia quotes and TV ... you name it!

1. Which PDC star owns a chip shop in South Wales?
2. Who said this, "So my mum decided one night to just run away with me to London when I was only three. It was obviously a very difficult time for her but that's the only reason I left Scotland."
3. On the TV show *Bullseye*, what total did the guest darts thrower need to reach to get the contestants' charity money doubled?
4. What is the black, log-end smaller dartboard more commonly known as?
5. Who said, "If you're going to be two-faced, at least make one of them pretty"?
6. What is 'Qualifying School'?
7. What was Wayne Mardle's walk-on music?
8. What is German player Kevin Munch also known as?
9. Which PDC darts referee is known as 'The Voice'?
10. Joe Cullen's walk-on music is which Oasis classic?

Quiz 23

The Nine-darters Quiz.

These are the historic throws that light up a tournament – they are few and far between but when they happen, wow! See how much you know about nine-dart finishes ...

1. Which year was the first televised nine-dart finish in PDC history?
    a. 2000
    b. 2001
    c. 2002.
2. Who threw the above nine-darter?
3. What was the final double of that first nine-darter?
    a. 10
    b. 12.
4. How many televised PDC nine-darters did Phil Taylor throw?
5. In 2010, there were two nine-dart finishes in the same match. Phil Taylor was one of the players, but who was the other?
6. In 2017, who was the first player to score two nine-dart finishes in the same match during a UK Open qualifier?
7. In 2013, aged 23, who became the youngest player (at the time) to achieve a nine-dart finish?
8. As of June 2025, how many televised nine-dart finishes had Luke Littler achieved?
9. And as of June 2025, how many televised nine-darters had Luke Humphries managed?
10. True or false – James Wade had made the same amount of televised nine-dart finishes as of June 2025 as Luke Littler and Luke Humphries combined?

Quiz 24

The Walk-On Music Quiz – Part 2.

Some banging tunes here for our darts stars – can you link them all up correctly?

1. Who walks on to The Killers' song, 'Mr Brightside'?
2. Who arrives on stage to 'I Predict A Riot' by The Kaiser Chiefs?
3. Which player walks on to 'Jump Around' by House of Pain?
4. Whose walk-on music is 'Eye of the Tiger' by Survivor?
5. Name the player who has 'Titanium' by Cia played as he walks on?
6. 'Don't Stop the Party' by Pitbull – whose walk-on song is that?
7. Can you name Luke Littler's walk-on song?
8. As of early 2025, which PJ & Duncan hit does Chris Dobey walk out to?
9. Michael Smith's walk-on song is ... ?
10. Jonny Clayton has chosen a walk-on song that includes his first name. What is the song?

Quiz 25

The PDC Hall of Fame Quiz.

The PDC Hall of Famers – who are they? Let's see how much you know about these legends of the game ...

1. When was the PDC Hall of Fame first launched?
2. Who were the first two darts legends inducted into the PDC Hall of Fame?
3. Sid Waddell and Dave Lanning were inducted when?
    a. 2006
    b. 2007
    c. 2008.
4. Who was the first Canadian to be inducted?
5. Which darts commentary legend was inducted in 2014?
    a. Stuart Pyke
    b. John Gwynne.
6. Which highly regarded referee entered the Hall of Fame in 2024?
7. The PDC Chairman was inducted in 2021. Who was it?
8. Which multiple World Champion was inducted in 2011?
9. What role did 2013 inductee Bruce Spendley have in the game?
10. The first PDC World Champion was inducted in 2009. Who was it?

Quiz 26

The Brainteaser Quiz

Here's a test of your darts smarts – see how quickly you can get through these ten questions ...

1. What's the lowest number than cannot be scored with one dart?
2. The Bullshooter World Championship electronic dart tournament is held annually in which city?
    a. Chicago
    b. New York.
3. Which nation did Co Stompe represent?
4. In which 2024 competition did Luke Littler achieve a nine-dart finish in the very first leg of a quarter-final against Nathan Aspinall?
5. On 23 September 2020, which PDC legend came out of retirement and announced his intention to compete in Qualifying School?
6. Who is the 'Demolition Man'?
7. Who beat Luke Humphries 11–10 to win the 2024 UK Open?
8. Who denied Phil Taylor a 17th World Championship title in the 2018 final?
9. After losing to Daryl Gurney at the 2024 World Championship, who announced that he would retire at the end of the year?
10. What did Gerwyn Price wear briefly during a World Championship quarter-final against Gabriel Clemens in 2023?

Quiz 27

The Guess Who Quiz.

Which darts players are being indicated below by our subtle and not-so subtle clues..?

1. A pint of cider and lager...
2. Three diamonds on a slot machine.
3. The player most likely to celebrate with a kebab?
4. The Barney Army would follow this player?
5. The Green Giant who is not always jolly?
6. Beachy Head could be another way of saying this player's nickname?
7. A measure of electricity could reveal this player's identity?
8. Delivering calves on a farm is how this player got his nickname?
9. This mythical giant gorilla once climbed the Empire State Building – but what is the nickname and player?
10. A London bus nickname for this player?

Quiz 28

The Scores on the Doors Quiz.

This set of ten questions is all about World Championship finals...

1. What score did Leighton Rees beat John Lowe in the first ever final?
   a. 11-7
   b. 12-6.
2. Who did Raymond van Barneveld beat to become World Champion for the first time?
3. Who won the PDC World Darts Championship in 2021?
4. How many 'whitewashes' did Phil Taylor achieve in World Championship finals?
5. True or false – Phil Taylor achieved back-to-back 7-0 final wins in 2001 and 2002?
6. How many of Phil Taylor's five final losses ended 7-6?
7. How many successive finals did Gary Anderson appear in?
8. By what score did Luke Humphries beat Luke Littler in the 2024 final?
9. True or False – Michael van Gerwen's 2025 final loss was his third in a row?
10. Who lost two of his World Championship finals by a score of 7-0?

Quiz 29

Legends Quiz: Dennis Priestley.

He carved his name into history and plenty more besides – find out why by answering the below set of ten ...

1. True or false – Dennis was the first ever PDC World Champion?
2. What's his nickname?
3. What is his walk-on music?
4. In the 1991 BDO World Championship, which fellow darts legend did he beat 6-0 in the final?
5. What did Dennis do before he became a darts pro?
    a. Newsagent
    b. Estate Agent.
6. He also worked as a what – a coal merchant or college janitor?
7. What is Priestley's highest PDC world ranking?
8. After three successive defeats in the final, which tournament did Dennis consider his 'bogey' event?
9. Which darting legend described Priestley as his darts 'soul mate'?
10. Which football team does Dennis support?
    a. Barnsley
    b. Leeds United
    c. Huddersfield Town.

Quiz 30

The TV Arrows Quiz.

These shows have all played a huge part in making darts as popular as it is today – can you get all ten correct?

1. Which pub-based 1970s TV show regularly featured darts?
2. True or false – Commentator John Gwynne was a Manchester City fan?
3. What was the 2024 Sky Documentaries series about darts called?
4. Stuart Pyke and John Gwynne both used to commentate for which Manchester radio station?
5. Stuart Pyke specifically used to commentate on which Greater Manchester football team?
    a. Bolton Wanderers
    b. Oldham Athletic.
6. Which year did Pyke join *Sky Sports*?
    a. 1999
    b. 2002
    c. 2004.
7. True or false – John Gwynne commentated on the first ever PDC World Championship in 1994?
8. How many unaired pilot shows of *Bullseye* were made before the classic TV show launched?
    a. 1
    b. 2
    c. 3.
9. Which classic TV soap opera regularly featured characters playing darts?
10. Dave Spikey presented a relaunched version of *Bullseye* in 2006, but in which cult Peter Kay comedy did he first make his name?

Quiz 31

True or False Eric Bristow Quiz.

How much do you know about the legend known simply as the 'Crafty Cockney'? The below questions are either true or false – see how many you can get:

1. He was born in Bow in London?
2. His walk-on music was Rabbit by Chas & Dave?
3. He beat Bobby George to claim his first World Championship in 1980?
4. He took his nickname from a pub of the same name?
5. Bristow once threw consecutive nine-dart finishes in a televised event in 1977
6. He won the World Cup singles four times?
7. He was Phil Taylor's mentor?
8. Eric was a huge Manchester United fan?
9. He suffered from several bouts of 'Dartitis'?
10. He once won 'I'm a Celebrity, Get Me Out of Here'?

Quiz 32

Jobs for the Boys.

Some of the most famous players in the world started out with ordinary day jobs. Can you figure out who did what? We're giving you two options to help ...

1. Phil Taylor – barman or traffic warden?
2. Raymond van Barneveld – bus driver or postman?
3. James Wade – car mechanic or milkman?
4. Wayne Mardle – lion tamer or accountant?
5. Jocky Wilson – stableboy or coalminer?
6. John Lowe – policeman or carpenter?
7. Luke Littler – ballboy or schoolboy?
8. Gerwyn Price – rugby player or bouncer?
9. Peter Wright – tyre fitter or hairdresser?
10. Jonny Clayton – driving instructor or plasterer?

Quiz 33

The World Cup of Darts Quiz – Part 1.

It's a PDC global contest that seems to grow in stature year on year. Let's see how much you know about the World Cup of Darts ...

1. How many nations competed at the World Cup of Darts as of 2025?
2. How many players does each nation have representing them?
3. Which year was the first PDC World Cup of Darts held?
4. Who were the first pair to win?
    a. Raymond van Barneveld and Co Stompé
    b. Mark Webster and Barrie Bates.
5. How many finals has Peter Wright appeared in?
6. Which English pair won four of the first six World Cup finals?
7. Which nation beat England pair Luke Littler and Luke Humphries at the 2025 World Cup?
8. With should be four losses, which nation has been runner-up the most as of 2025?
9. True or false – Michael Smith has won two World Cup titles as of 2025?
10. Of the 11 World Cup tournaments held in Germany, which city has hosted the event more?
    a. Hamburg
    b. Frankfurt.

Quiz 34

Record Breakers.

This set of ten is all about the record-breakers – the darts players that set the bar higher than the rest by surpassing their peers ...

1. As of 2025, who is the holder of the highest televised average, of 123.40?
2. In 1984, darts legend John Lowe became the first player to achieve a televised what?
3. Which player hit 24 maximums (180) in a single match during the 2017 PDC World Championship final against Michael van Gerwen?
4. Which player hit a world record for a televised leg of just 38 seconds during a UK Open match in 2012, hitting 180, 177, and then checking out 144 for a nine-dart finish?
5. With a total of 11, who has achieved the most nine-dart finishes for televised events?
6. In 1978, Leighton Rees became the first recognised what in darts?
7. Who is the youngest player to win a PDC World Championship?
8. What is the fewest amount of darts needed to win five darts legs?
9. Who was the first player to throw a nine-dart finish in a PDC World Championship final?
10. What average did Phil Taylor achieve in the group phase of the the 2012 Premier League?
    a. 107.60
    b. 106.45
    c. 105.25

Quiz 35

The (Even More) Nicknames Quiz.

From the flattering nicknames to the borderline insulting – here's another ten nickname puzzles to solve ...

1. Who is nicknamed 'Voltage'?
2. What is the rather unflattering nickname of Daryl Gurney?
3. Who is also known as 'The German Giant'?
4. Can you name who 'Bully Boy' is?
5. Who is known as 'The Machine'?
6. Who is better known as the 'Queen of the Palace'?
7. 'Jackpot' is the nickname of which former World Champion?
8. Damon Heta uses an anagram of his surname for his nickname – what is it?
9. 'Hollywood' is whose nickname?
10. Dave Chisnall's nickname is what?

Quiz 36

The More About Sid Waddell Quiz.

Time to take the microphone again and find out more about the legend that was Sid Waddell.

1. Which football club did Sid support?
2. What was Sid better known as?
3. Which Northumberland town was Sid born in?
    a. Alnwick
    b. Seahouses.
4. Sid's legendary corny lines also led him to be nicknamed what?
5. Which year did Sid start commentating for *Sky Sports*?
    a. 1992
    b. 1993
    c. 1994.
6. True or false – Sid was once nominated for a BAFTA?
7. What was the series of children's cricket books Sid wrote called?
8. True or false – Sid wrote a novel in 1975 that was banned by some high street newsagents?
9. Which year was the PDC World Championship darts trophy renamed 'The Sid Waddell Trophy'?
10. Which singing legend did Sid once claim, "The atmosphere is so tense, if (*****) walked in with a portion of chips, you could hear the vinegar sizzle on them."

Quiz 37

Who Said That?

Here are some memorable quotes from players from the past and present. Can you figure out who is speaking?

1. "I've got a nice little crafty deal with the people in Barbados; ten days out there teaching the locals how to play darts for an hour a day. Get paid for that as well."
    a. Eric Bristow
    b. Jocky Wilson.
2. "All this cuddling and kissing on stage these days, well it's all right in football when someone scores a goal, but not when you're playing darts."
    a. Eric Bristow
    b. Cliff Lazarenko.
3. "Well as giraffes say, you don't get no leaves unless you stick your neck out."
    a. Sid Waddell
    b. Tony Green.
4. "Darts in 1965, well you used to hit a 180 and get a free pint in the pub! With those darts though, you needed it."
    a. Jocky Wilson
    b. Bobby George.
5. "Before a match I like to relax with 25 bottles of Holsten Pils and six steak and kidney pies."
    a. Andy Fordham
    b. Jocky Wilson.
6. "It's in his genes – it's in his 501s. Cushty-wushty."
    a. Sid Waddell
    b. Bobby George.
7. "Cliff Lazarenko's idea of exercise is a firm press on a soda siphon."
    a. Sid Waddell
    b. Bobby George.

8. "My wife says, 'I'm not half the man I used to be', and she's not kidding."
    a. Andy Fordham
    b. Jocky Wilson.
9. "I'm not arrogant, I'm just better."
    a. Phil Taylor
    b. Eric Bristow.
10. "The crowd is fantastic. They either boo you or cheer you. Either way, it's great."
    a. Peter Wright
    b. Michael van Gerwen.

Question 10: Peter Wright or Michael van Gerwen?

Quiz 38

Legends Quiz: John Part.

The Canadian PDC legend and *Sky Sports* commentator John Part is the latest subject of our darts greats quiz focus ...

1. Where was John born?
    a. Montreal
    b. Toronto
    c. Ottawa.
2. How many PDC World Championships has he won?
3. True or false – Part is a five-time runner-up in the World Grand Prix, World Matchplay and UK Open?
4. How many Canadian Open titles did he win?
    a. 1
    b. 2
    c. 3.
5. Which year did Part join *Sky Sports*' commentary team?
    a. 2011
    b. 2013.
6. How many televised nine-dart finishes did Part achieve?
7. What was his highest world ranking?
8. What was his best World Cup of Darts finish?
    a. 2nd round
    b. Quarter-final
    c. Winner.
9. True or false – Part is statistically the greatest North American darts player or all time?
10. His nickname is 'Darth' what?:
    a. Vadar
    b. Maple
    c. Maul.

Quiz 39

The World Cup of Darts Quiz – Part 2.

More on the World Cup – and this one's a bit tougher!

1. Which country won the PDC World Cup in 2023?
2. Which two players represented the PDC World Cup winners in 2023?
3. What year was the World Cup of Darts first held?
4. Which nation has won the competition the most (as of 2025)?
5. The Netherlands have won the World Cup how many times?
    a. 2
    b. 4.
6. How many World Cup finals has Michael van Gerwen featured in?
    a. 2
    b. 4
    c. 6.
7. How many times has Jonny Clayton won the World Cup?
8. How many times has Phil Taylor reached the World Cup final?
9. True or false – Belgium has never won the World Cup?
10. Which is the only non-European nation to win the World Cup?

Quiz 40

Stand Up if You Love Ally Pally!

It's the iconic venue that hosts the PDC World Championship over the festive period each year. Let's see what your 'Ally Pally' knowledge is like!

1. When was the first PDC World Championship held at Alexandra Palace?
    a. 2005/06 event
    b. 2007/08 event.
2. Which year did Fallon Sherrock become known as 'The Queen of the Palace'?
3. As of the 2025 event, approximately how many darts fans attend the event in total?
    a. 70,000
    b. 80,000
    c. 90,000.

4. Which song is played during breaks and at the end of games during the tournament?
    a. 'Chase the Sun' by Planet Funk
    b. 'Setting Sun' by The Chemical Brothers.
5. Approximately how many pints of beer are drunk at each event?
    a. 250,000
    b. 500,000
    c. 750,000.
6. Where is Alexandra Palace?
    a. London
    b. Manchester
    c. Birmingham.
7. When was the venue first opened?
    a. 1873
    b. 1973.
8. Approximately how far is 'Ally Pally' away from Wembley Stadium?
    a. 10 miles
    b. 50 miles
    c. 100 miles.
9. Alexandra Palace's West Hall, which plays host to the PDC World Darts Championship, boasts a capacity of how many?
    a. 2,500
    b. 3,000
    c. 3,500.
10. Which legendary singer termed the phrase 'Ally Pally'?
    a. Dame Gracie Fields
    b. Dame Vera Lynn.

Quiz 41

The Darts Pioneers Quiz – Part 2.

The *News of the World* Championship was one of the biggest events in darts' embryonic years. Here are ten questions to test your knowledge.

1. The championship ran from what years?
    a. 1915-1965
    b. 1927-1997
    c. 1945-1990.
2. Which player won the final championship?
    a. John Lowe
    b. Leighton Rees
    c. Phil Taylor.
3. True or false – The *News of the World* was a Sunday newspaper?
4. *Sky Sports* covered the event just once in 1997 – is that true?
5. Who claimed, "You're not a proper world champion until you've won the *News of the World*."
6. What was unique about Stefan Lord becoming champion in 1977/78?
7. True or false – John Lowe never won the tournament?
8. In its 70 years of existence, how many women's *News of the World* championships were there?
    a. 0
    b. 2
    c. 70.
9. What was the estimated number of contestants at the first event in 1927?
    a. 100
    b. 500
    c. 1,000.
10. How many times did Eric Bristow win the event?

Quiz 42

The Before They Were Famous Quiz.

Here are some more everyday jobs darts players used to do before they became pros ...

1. Andrew Gilding used to be a:
    a. Butcher
    b. Baker
    c. Candlestick maker.
2. What stylising job did Ryan Meikle once do?
3. Mensur Suljović once ran what sort of shop with his brothers?
    a. Coffee shop
    b. Chip shop
    c. Pet shop.
4. Florian Hempel was a professional sportsman before he turned to darts. What was the sport?
5. Brendan Dolan's previous occupation would be very handy to householders. Was he a plumber, painter & decorator or gardener?
6. Rob Cross' nickname Voltage is a clue to his former profession. What was his profession?
7. Michael Smith's nickname of 'Bully Boy' is actually a good clue to his former job. What was it?
8. Which trade did Cameron Menzies work in before turning pro?
    a. Plumber
    b. Gardener
    c. Estate agent.
9. Can you guess what Luke Littler was before becoming a darts superstar?
10. Where did Scott Williams once work?
    a. Warehouse
    b. Public House
    c. Pizza Hut.

Quiz 43

The When Darts Goes Wrong Quiz.

Even the fun yet competitive sport that darts is has its occasional spat. See if you can work out who were the targets of these toxic tantrums...

1. Adrian Lewis had this to say about who? "He said after his previous match that I was going to crumble against him, but a two-time World Champion doesn't do that. Tonight, I didn't crumble, he crumbled."
2. Who was Adrian Lewis spitting venom at when he said, "He's a big mouth who's never won anything and never will win anything."
3. Adrian Lewis again... who is the intended target of this? "The reflection there was that I was rubbish and that just shows why he is a nobody, simple as that."
4. Who aimed this at the 2021 World Grand Prix audience? "The crowd are a bit rubbish again, as you can hear, but I won so no matter what they do I'll keep winning. The crowd are absolutely pathetic, but I won."
5. Who is Gerwyn Price on about here? "I don't know what was going through his head."
6. Who said this of Adrian Lewis in 2020? "I didn't overstep the mark. To be honest, half the time I didn't need to do anything, all I had to do was say things like 'watch out, you don't know what I'm going to do' during this game."
7. Who is commentator Wayne Mardle on about here? "There's genuine aggression between these two."
    a. Adrian Lewis v Gerwyn Price
    b. Peter Wright v Peter Manley.
8. Who said this about Michael van Gerwen? "The only reason he got the hump with me was because I gave it large. I said 'well, you do it every week' so you've got to expect a bit back."

Adrian Lewis

9. Adrian Lewis – again – who is he having a dig at here? "If he wants to be a clown, let him get on with it."
10. Who said this of Adrian Lewis's winding up during a World Cup match? "Adrian was on me the whole tournament. Even when we weren't playing, he was going on about how I shouldn't be playing for Australia. When he puts the England shirt on, he becomes a very different person."

Quiz 44

The Make Mine a Double Quiz.

The double is most often the way a player finishes in a game of 501 – but doubles, trebles and their variants all have their own nicknames. How many can you figure out?

1. What double is known as 'Annie's Room'?
2. Which double is known as 'Basement'?
3. What is a 'Champagne Finish'?
4. Which double is sometimes called 'Dinky Doo'?
5. A score of 33 is also known as what?
6. A score of 77 is nicknamed what?
    a. Sunset Strip
    b. Santa Monica Boardwalk.
7. The same score (77) is also known as something people use to keep dry in the rain. What is it called?
8. What is a 'Motown Finish'?
9. The bingo term 'Two Fat Ladies' is also used in darts. What score does it represent?
10. A score of 57 is known as what?

Quiz 45

That's Darts Quiz.

Bits and pieces of darts trivia that will get you scratching your head!

1. What is 'Dartitis'?
2. True or false – 'Dartitis' is a recognised medical condition?
3. What does it mean when a 'marker' is thrown?
4. When a player is called a 'Carolina Leaner', what are they likely to be doing?
5. What does 'Cracked' refer to in darts?
6. 'Iron Man' means to do what?
7. When would a 'Match dart' be thrown?
8. When three darts are so tightly bunched that at least one flight pops off, what is that known as?
9. If you hear 'splitting the 11' after a shot, where is the dart likely to have landed?
10. How much is a 'Baby Ton' worth?

Quiz 46

Legends Quiz: Keith Deller.

One of darts early stars, Keith Deller's name was synonymous with televised darts during his heyday, so let's learn more about him!

1. Deller had three nicknames including 'The Fella'. Can you name one of the other two?
2. When was Deller crowned BDO World Champion?
    a. 1981
    b. 1983.
3. Who did he beat in the above final?
4. True or false – Deller is the only World Champion ever to have beaten the top three ranked players along the way?
5. Where was Deller born?
    a. Ipswich
    b. Norwich.
6. Was Deller left or right-handed?
7. True or false – Deller was a founding member of the PDC?
8. Deller walked on to which 1990s hit by D:Ream?
9. Deller held the *Guinness* World Record for the fastest three legs of 301 in how many seconds?
    a. 93
    b. 97
    c. 101.
10. Deller was honoured in 2024 for his charitable work. Did he receive:
    a. OBE
    b. CBE
    c. MBE.

Quiz 47

The PDC Prize Money Quiz.

Prize money pots, winner's purses and everything else money-related!

1. How much did Luke Littler win for becoming 2025 PDC World Champion?
2. How much will the 2025/26 World Championship winner receive?
    a. £500,000
    b. £750,000
    c. £1m.
3. How much will the Premier League winner get in 2025/26?
    a. £350,000
    b. £400,000.
4. True or false – The World Matchplay winner will receive £200,000?
5. The Grand Slam of Darts winner receives more than the World Matchplay winner – is that true?
6. The World Grand Prix winner gets how much?
    a. £150,000
    b. £175,000
    c. £190,000.
7. How much is the 2025/26 World Championship prize fund?
    a. £2.5m
    b. £3.75m
    c. £5m.
8. What is winning the European Championships worth – more or less than £200,000?
9. Which winner's pot is greater – the UK Open or World Masters?
10. True or false – The winners of the 2025 World Cup of Darts receive £80,000 between them?

Quiz 48

Location, Location, Location.

Time to take a geography trip around the UK. Let's find out how much you know about where the top players come from ...

1. What is the name of Luke Littler's hometown?
2. Where is Luke Humphries's hometown?
3. Aldershot is the home town of who?
    a. James Wade
    b. Peter Wright.
4. Where is Stephen Bunting's hometown?
5. Which player lives in Hastings?
    a. Rob Cross
    b. Gary Anderson.
6. Who was born in Markham, South Wales?
7. Llanelli is known as a great rugby town, but which top darts player was born there?
8. True or false – Peter Wright was born in Edinburgh?
9. Which past master hails from Stoke-on-Trent?
10. Nathan Aspinall comes from which Greater Manchester town?
    a. Bury
    b. Stockport.

Quiz 49

Darts Players and Football – Part 1.

Darts and football – two games of the working class and therefore a match made in heaven. Here are ten questions for when the two sports cross paths ...

1. Which Tottenham player and darts fan celebrates by pretending to throw a dart?
2. Which football team does Alan 'Chuck' Norris support?
    a. Liverpool
    b. Manchester City.
3. Who does Luke Littler follow?
4. Luke Humphries follows a team known as 'The Whites'. Who are they?
5. Nathan Aspinall follows a team from Manchester. Who is it? City or United?
6. Gary Anderson follows one of Edinburgh's biggest sides – but is it Hearts or Hibernian?
7. Chris Dobey's accent might give you a clue to which club from the North East he supports?
8. Adrian Lewis follows a team known as 'The Potters'. Who are they?
9. Michael van Gerwen follows a Dutch side once associated with electronic giants Philips. Who is the team?
10. Stephen Bunting is a dyed-in-the-wool 'Red' – but which 'Red' is it?
    a. Manchester United
    b. Liverpool.

Quiz 50

Darts Players and Football – Part 2.

And here are another ten on darts and football ...

1. Dave Chisnall supports one of the Merseyside giants – but is it Everton or Liverpool?
2. Raymond van Barneveld supports a Dutch side that you can figure out from this anagram – HAND AGE.
3. Wayne Mardle's team are known for 'marching in' – but is it Southampton or Tottenham?
4. Phil Taylor and pop star Robbie Williams both support this lower league Potteries team. Can you name the team?
5. Michael Smith is one of several darts players to support this world famous club – but is it Liverpool or Manchester United?
6. Jonny Clayton also supports one of the above two clubs – is it the same as 'Bully Boy'?
7. Rob Cross is a fan of this fashionable club in West London.
8. Peter Wright follows an English side nicknamed 'The Canaries', but who are they?
9. Joe Cullen's walk-on music is by Oasis, who support the rivals of the club he loves! Which club is it?
10. Dimitri Van den Bergh is a fan of one of these top Belgian sides – but which one?
    a. Royal Antwerp
    b. Anderlecht.

Quiz 51

The History Makers.

More players that have left an indelible mark on darts ...

1. Who did Fallon Sherrock beat 3–2 in the first round of the 2019 PDC World Championships?
2. Who denied Phil Taylor a 17th world darts title in 2018?
3. Who, in 2011, became the first player to hit a nine-dart finish in a "double-to-start" event giving him the nickname "The History Maker"?
4. The most 180s in a tournament record was set at the 2024 PDC World Championship – was it:
    a. 914
    b. 920
    c. 929.
5. Who threw 83 maximum 180s in a single tournament in 2022?
6. Peter Wright and Michael Smith both hit a record number of 180s in separate matches, but how many was that?
    a. 20
    b. 22
    c. 24.
7. The 2017 World Championship final between Gary Anderson and Michael van Gerwen was a 180-fest with the most maximums scored in one game. But how many did they manage?
    a. 30
    b. 36
    c. 42.
8. Who hit a record set average of 140.91 at the 2025 World Championship?
9. Who, in 2003, became the first overseas winner of the PDC World Championship?
10. Who were the next two overseas winners of the title?

Quiz 52

Legends Quiz: Rob Cross.

The popular PDC star that is Rob Cross has been in and around the world's top ten for several years. How well do you the man they call ... actually, that's one of the questions below!

1. What is Rob's walk-on music?
2. Is Rob right or left-handed?
3. What year did Rob win the World Matchplay?
4. Which year did Rob finish runner-up at the UK Open?
5. As of 2025, what was his highest world ranking?
    a. 1
    b. 2
    c. 3.
6. Of the 11 major PDC finals Rob has reached how many times has he finished runner-up?
7. Rob won the World Championship in 2018, but who did he beat?
8. Who was Rob's partner in the 2020 World Cup of Darts?
    a. Michael Smith
    b. Stephen Bunting.
9. How many televised nine-dart finishes has Rob achieved?
    a. 1
    b. 3
    c. 5.
10. Who did Rob beat in the final of the 2021 PDC European Championships?

Quiz 53

The Stephen Bunting Quiz.

Let's get going with ten brainteasers on the popular big man ...

1. What is the fan chant that often accompanies Stephen on stage?
2. What was Stephen's old walk-on song (before 'Titanium')?
3. Which rugby team does he follow?
4. Which Family Guy character was Stephen often associated with?
5. What social media platform is he particularly active on?
    a. X
    b. Instagram
    c. TikTok.
6. Which year did he win the PDC Masters?
7. As of 2025, how many World Championship semi-finals had he reached?
8. Which year was he crowned BDO World Champion?
9. What is the home ground of Stephen's favourite football team?
10. In 2001 he won what?
    a. World Youth Masters
    b. British Teenage Open
    c. Both a + b.

Quiz 54

Who Said It.

We all love a memorable quote but see if you can figure out who said the ten statements below – there are clues if you can fish them out!

1. Who once said, "I may change my darts, my hair, or my outfit, but one thing that never changes is my love for the game."
2. "Jocky Wilson ... what an athlete!"
3. "I made Phil Taylor a monster – the thrashing I gave him made him the player he became."
4. "I practice for like, half an hour to 45 minutes a day."
5. "The games you lose are the games you always remember."
6. "Listen, I am the best player in the world!"
7. "Peter (Wright) played crap. I can have a big mouth now, but with a 92 average you need to shut your mouth and get back to the practice board."
8. "Darts players are probably fitter than most footballers in overall body strength."
9. "I like to be different, to be my own person, and darts allows me to express myself."
10. "I always believe in myself, no matter what. You have to have confidence to win."

Quiz 55

Legends Quiz: John Lowe

Perhaps the first superstar of darts, here are ten questions on the great John Lowe and his many achievements ...

1. What was Lowe's walk-on music?
2. True or false – Lowe threw the first televised nine-darter?
3. How much did Lowe earn for his first nine-dart finish (televised)?
    a. 52,000
    b. 77,000
    c. 102,000.
4. What was the title of Lowe's 2005 autobiography?
    a. Old Stoneface
    b. Highs and Lowes.
5. How many years did Lowe appear at the World Championship?
    a. 24
    b. 26
    c. 28.
6. Lowe is a supporter of which football club?
    a. Sunderland
    b. Middlesbrough
    c. Newcastle United.
7. True or false – Lowe was the guest on an unaired pilot of hit ITV show *Bullseye?*
8. Lowe was previously a what?
    a. Painter
    b. Plasterer
    c. Carpenter.
9. True or false – Lowe's son is a professional darts player?
10. Who said this, "To be a champion, you have to believe in yourself when no one else will."
    a. Phil Taylor
    b. John Lowe.

Quiz 56

The Luke or Luke Quiz.

Luke Littler or Luke Humphries – which of these two darts superstars said the following?

1. "Probably going to Bahrain last week and winning that tournament with not even ten minutes of practice."
2. "Comeback is always greater than the setback."
3. "I don't have any GCSEs; everyone probably has more than me. Although I did pass my sport."
4. "It's important to be open about mental health issues and not be afraid to bring the subject up."
5. "I've had an obsession with having a heart attack, worrying if it's beating fine and that's where my anxiety spiralled from."
6. "I have certainly broken the rules and records already, but I know if my game is there I can beat even more records. I think I am daring to dream now. I am only three wins away."
7. "It feels that much greater because of the adversity that I've gone through."
8. "That's my mate's place and they've now got the 'Luke Wrap' under my name. I walked in yesterday and got a burger and chips. They showed me two orders for my wraps, and they've now got to replace the big doner meat every three days. They've also got a barber's shop, Hamidos, so they give me free haircuts now."
9. "To get to play in one of the most iconic venues and to get to that quarter-final, it's a feeling that will never fade away."
10. "There was nothing to talk to myself about before playing Michael for the first time. You've got to think you're going to beat whoever's in front of you."

Quiz 57

The Nine-darters Quiz.

Here's another set of ten on the Holy Grail of all darts players – the nine-dart finish ...

1. Who in 2006 became the first player to hit three tournament nine-dart finishes in a calendar year?
2. Who achieved the first ever televised nine-darter?
3. The first nine-dart finish at the BDO World Championships came in 1990, but who threw it?
4. As of June 2025, who was the only player to throw two televised nine-darters in the same match?
5. Who was the first player to hit a nine-darter in a World Championship final?
6. Who was the second player to achieve a nine-dart finish in a World Championship final?
7. Who became the first woman to throw a televised nine-dart finish in 2023?
8. Who is the youngest player to hit a televised nine-darter?
9. What is meant by a nine-dart 'outshot?
    a. a dart out of the board
    b. the final three darts of the nine
10. True or false – Alan 'Chuck' Norris hit a nine-darter against Michael Smith in the 2016 Players Championship Finals?

Quiz 58

The General Legends Quiz.

This quiz could be about any darts legend – it's non-specific and a good test of your powers ...

1. Whose death was sadly announced during a 2018 match between Peter Wright and Daryl Gurney?
2. Phil Taylor reached the final of all 14 PDC World Darts Championship tournaments held at which Essex venue?
3. Which darts legend won the World Championship in three different decades?
4. Which darts giant of yesteryear used to walk out "All Right Now' by Free?
5. Who did *Top of the Pops* (allegedly) mistakenly use a picture of during a huge Dexy's Midnight Runners appearance?
6. Which darts pioneer used to walk on stage dressed in a crown and cloak holding a candelabra?
7. Which darts icon mentored Phil Taylor?
8. Keith Deller holds the *Guiness* World Record for the fastest three legs of 301. Was his time:
    a. 97 seconds
    b. 117 seconds
    c. 137 seconds.
9. Which three-time World Championn was known as 'Darth Maple'?
10. How many major PDC finals has Raymond van Barneveld appeared in?
    a. 10
    b. 15
    c. 20.

Quiz 59

Legends Quiz: Peter Manley

The controversial, larger than life darts legend that is Peter Manley is now under the spotlight ...

1. How many times was Manley a runner-up in the PDC World Championship?
2. Who did he lose to on each occasion?
3. What did commentator Tony Green nickname Manley?
4. What was his original walk-on music?
5. What music did he change to?
6. Can you name the one televised PDC event Manley won?
7. Manley was best man at which fellow darts player's wedding?
    a. Wayne Mardle
    b. Phil Taylor.
8. How many years did Manley spend as PDC world ranked No.1?
    a. 0 years
    b. 1 year
    c. 2 years.
9. True or false – Manley is lifelong Manchester City supporter?
10. Out of 22 sets he played in during his three PDC World Championship finals, how many did Manley win?
    a. 1
    b. 2
    c. 3.

Quiz 60

The More Walk-on Music Quiz.

You know the tunes all too well, but do you know the players who walk out to them?

1. Who walks out to 'Play Hard' by David Guetta?
2. What is James Wade's walk-on music?
3. Ross Smith walks out to which Billy Ocean classic?
4. Which heavy metal anthem does Ryan Searle walk on to?
5. Daryl Gurney's walk-on theme is guaranteed to get the crowd singing, but what is it?
6. William O'Connor walks out to which Cranberries classic?
7. 'I Don't Wanna Wait' by David Guetta is the walk-on music for which player?
8. Dave Chisnall has a comedy legend singing his theme, but who is it?
9. Fallon Sherrock walks out to 'Last Friday Night', but who sings it?
10. There's only one song Gerwyn Price could choose given his nickname, but which song is it?

Quiz 61

The PDC – How Much Do You Know?

The PDC have made darts a multimillion pound worldwide sport – let's find out more about this well-oiled and progressive organisation ...

1. What does PDC stand for?
2. Who is the PDC chairman?
3. When was the PDC first established? 1992 or 1994?
4. Can you name four of the PDC's major competitions?
5. What was the PDC formerly known as?
6. Where are the PDC headquarters based?
    a. Brentwood
    b. Fulham.
7. Who was the first PDC World Champion in 1994?
8. Who was the first PDC World Championship runner-up?
9. How much was the prize money at the 2025 PDC World Championships?
    a. £1.5m
    b. £2.5m.
10. Which broadcaster covered the first major PDC event?
    a. Sky Sports
    b. *Anglia TV.*

Quiz 62

The Even More Nicknames Quiz – Legends Special.

These might be a breeze as you go through them with ease – nicknames of the high and mighty – we're expecting you to hit a bullseye with these ten!

1. Who was known as 'The Crafty Cockney'?
2. Which former world champion was nicknamed 'The Power'?
3. Who is affectionately known as 'Barney'?
4. Which legend was unflatteringly known as 'Old Stoneface'?
5. Can you name the player known as 'Hawaii 501'?
6. Who was known as 'The Menace'?
7. Andy Fordham's nickname has Nordic warrior origins. Can you name it?
8. Jose de Sousa shares his nickname with football manager Jose Mourinho. Can you name it?
9. Who was known as 'Double Dekker'?
10. The 'King of Bling' was who?

Quiz 63

Darts Terminology and Slang A-Z – Part 1.

You night have heard these phrases, but what do they actually mean?

1. What other name for darts might interest Robin Hood?
2. If the first two darts aren't high scoring, what is a final dart treble also known as?
3. What is the nickname of a score of 26 when getting a single one, single five and single 20?
4. What is a 170 checkout of treble 20, treble 20, bullseye better known as?
5. A nice easy one – what's the centre of a dartboard better known as?
6. What does 'bull up' mean?
7. If you score more points that your remaining total, you have done what?
8. Traditionally, what is used to keep score of a darts game in clubs and pubs up and down the land?
9. A big check-out also shares part of its name with an expensive bottle of bubbles. What is it?
10. Everyone knows the answer to this – the total number of points to win a leg, finishing with a double or bullseye is known as a what?

Quiz 64

The Even More Who Said This Quiz.

You know the drill, well-known or memorable lines said by who?

1. "The other day Phil was going on about how he could not get a set of table and chairs in his Bentley. What does he want a Bentley for? It is pathetic, absolutely pathetic."
2. "I drive a nine-year old car, and he rubs everyone's noses in it by driving round in a Bentley."
3. "Phil is lucky I'm not 10 years younger when my b*******s were bigger than my brain. He is always giving it the 'Bertie big.'"
4. Who said this about Dutchman Vincent van der Voort, "His darts used to stick out like tulips in the board."
5. "Painter didn't play well early on – you could say he was up and down like a paint brush."
6. "Bristow reasons; Bristow quickens; aaaaah Bristow!"
7. "William Tell could take an apple off your head; Taylor could take out a processed pea."
8. "Darts really can help with literacy."
9. "I asked for the air-conditioning to be turned off, because it was blowing my darts all over the shop."
10. "Is ballroom dancing a sport? It's recognised as a sport but I don't see any balls there."

Quiz 65

Darts Terminology and Slang Quiz A-Z – Part 2.

Now there's a title for a quiz! As before – phrases and sayings – but what the heck do they mean?

1. What is meant by a 'combination finish'?
2. How many points is double top worth?
3. What is the standard starting score of a leg?
4. What board number double is connected to the phrase 'Madhouse'?
5. What is the fewest amount of darts required to win a 501 leg?
6. At seven feet, nine and a quarter inches away from the front of the dartboard, what is the marked throwing area limit better known as?
7. It's rare, but what is a 'Robin Hood' in darts?
8. A 'Shanghai' finish means what?
9. What does a 'bag of nails' or 'bucket of nails' mean in darts?
10. What is the decorative plastic designed part of a dart better known as?

Quiz 66

The Greatest Darts Show Ever Quiz?

Here are ten questions on the classic ITV show *Bullseye* which still has a cult following to this day and has been remade on a few occasions over the years ...

1. Who was the original presenter of *Bullseye*?
2. Who was the scorer on the show?
3. What was the original show's mascot called?
4. Which year was *Bullseye* first aired?
    a. 1981
    b. 1982
    c. 1983.
5. What did winning contestants aim at to win prizes?
6. What would contestants win if they scored two darts in the same bed in the prize round?
7. How many series did Jim Bowen present?
    a. 10
    b. 12
    c. 14.
8. Name the two presenters who have fronted modern remakes?
9. What did Jim Bowen mean when he said contestants could end up with a BFH?
10. What would Jim Bowen say when contestants didn't win the star prize gamble?

Quiz 67

Legends Quiz: Gary Anderson.

The popular Scot has enjoyed a fantastic career. Let's find out more by answering these ten questions correctly ...

1. What is Anderson's highest world ranking?
   a. 1
   b. 2
   c. 3.
2. Which years did Gary win the PDC World Darts Championship?
3. How many PDC Premier League titles has he won?
   a. 2
   b. 4
   c. 5.
4. What did Gary previously work as?
   a. Baker
   b. Builder
   c. Barrister.
5. True or false – Gary once ran a pub with his wife?
6. Which Edinburgh football team does Gary follow?
   a. Hearts
   b. Hibs.
7. What nickname does Gary share with legend Jocky Wilson?
8. What was his first nickname?
9. How many televised nine-darters has Gary achieved as of June 2025?
10. Who knocked Anderson out of the 2025 World Championships?

Quiz 68

The All-England Quiz.

These players are all English, but can you name their hometowns or counties?

1. Chris Dobey – is he from Cumbria or Northumberland?
2. Rob Cross – is he from Kent or Middlesex?
3. Dave Chisnall is from a darts hotbed in Merseyside. Where is it?
4. Ross Smith – is he from Kent or Suffolk?
5. Ryan Searle – Somerset or Wiltshire?
6. Joe Cullen – Yorkshire or Lancashire?
7. Where is Ryan Joyce from – Sunderland or Newcastle?
8. Andrew Gilding – Suffolk or Norfolk?
9. Callan Rydz – does he call Sunderland, Middlesbrough or Newcastle his hometown?
10. Luke Woodhouse is from Worcestershire or Warwickshire?

Quiz 69

The We All Love A Bit More Bully Quiz.

More trivia and puzzles to solve about the best darts TV show ever ...

1. What did every *Bullseye* contestant leave with?
2. How many contestants competed on each show?
    a. 2
    b. 4
    c. 6.
3. Which TV region was *Bullseye* filmed in?
    a. Central
    b. Granada
    c. Tyne Tees.
4. Which of these star prizes was most common?
    a. Lawnmower
    b. Speedboat
    c. Jet Ski.
5. How many points did the winning pair need to score from six darts to win the star prize?
6. What was Jim Bowen's real name?
    a. Peter Williams
    b. James Bowman.
7. True or false – Jim Bowen claims he never once said, "Super, smashing, great" in one sentence?
8. The original *Bullseye* was screened most regularly on which night of the week?
9. How many viewers regularly tuned in?
    a. 5-10m
    b. 10-15m
    c. 15-20m.
10. Including adverts, how long did each episode of *Bullseye* last?

Quiz 70

Nicknames Quiz (again).

You know the drill by now – tell us what these players are better known as – or who these nicknames belong to ...

1. Who is Simon Whitlock better known as ?
2. Who is known as 'Duzza'?
3. Dimitri Van den Bergh is known as what?
4. Joe Cullen's nickname is what?
5. Who is also known as 'The Bullet'?
6. Steve Beaton is known as 'The Bronzed' what?
7. Can you name 'The German Giant'?
8. Ryan Searle's nickname sounds like an Ozzy Osbourne concert. What is it?
9. Can you name the makeup device Christian Kist is named after?
10. Cliff Lazerenko's name was apt considering his imposing height and frame. What was it?

Quiz 71

Darts Players and Their Football Teams.

More football and darts crossovers as we see who our favourite players follow (for their sins!).

1. Which Suffolk side does Keith Deller follow?
2. Damon Heta supports which former European champions?
3. Joe Cullen follows a team many darts players seem to support, but who is it?
4. Dirk van Duijvenbode is a follower of a Dutch side known for their 'Total Football'. Who are they?
5. Josh Rock is a fan of these Glasgow giants. Who are they?
6. Legendary referee Russ Bray's team are forever blowing bubbles. Who are they?
7. Alan Soutar follows which Scottish side known as 'The Smokies'?
8. Eric Bristow was a fan of which West London team?
9. John Lowe is a fan of this team nicknamed 'The Black Cats'. Who are they?
10. Sky Sports presenter Laura Woods follows which North London giant?

Quiz 72

Random Trivia Quiz.

A potpourri of darts trivia for you to get your teeth into ...

1. What is Beau Greaves' walk-on music?
2. 'Rhinestone Cowboy' by Glen Campbell is the walk-on music of who?
3. True or false – the youngest World Champion: Luke Littler was 17 years 11 months and 13 days when he won his first world title in 2025?
4. Phil Taylor was 52 years and five months old when he became what?
5. Which Right Said Fred smash hit did Andy Fordham walk out to?
6. Which Dutch darts star revealed he has attention deficit hyperactivity disorder (ADHD)?
7. What World Champions suffered from Dartitus?
8. True or false – Ryan Searle suffers from a condition called astigmatism?
9. Who once walked on to 'Let Me Entertain You' by Robbie Williams?
10. True or false – Phil Taylor's dog is called 'Bully'?

Quiz 73

The Iconic Venues Quiz.

More legendary darts venues to test your knowledge on ...

1. What is the current venue of the PDC World Darts Championship?
2. Which Purfleet venue was the home of the PDC World Darts Championship (1994-2007)?
3. Which iconic Blackpool venue is home to the PDC World Matchplay?
4. The BDO World Darts Championship was held here from 1986 to 2019?
5. Which 20,000-capacity venue in London hosts the PDC Premier League?
6. Which South West location and holiday resort hosts the PDC UK Open and Players Championship Finals?
7. Which Milton Keynes venue hosts the PDC Masters (now rebranded as the World Masters)?
8. Which Leicester location hosts the PDC World Grand Prix?
9. Which Northern Ireland venue hosts the PDC Premier League?
10. Wolverhampton hosts the PDC Grand Slam of Darts. Where is it?

Quiz 74

True or False Quiz.

Plain and simple – are these statements true or false, and here's the good news, you have a 50% chance of being right!

1. Darts is believed to have originated from archery?
2. Darts is a game that originated in the Netherlands?
3. A standard dartboard is also known as a 'clock face'?
4. A regulation dartboard is 20 inches in diameter?
5. The first recorded indoor darts match took place in 1908?
6. The highest checkout in darts is 166?
7. Darts is played in more than 100 countries?
8. There is a well-known darts game called badminton?
9. If a dart bounces out of the board, the player can take another go?
10. In years gone by, many darts professionals drank beer and smoked cigarettes during matches?

Quiz 75

General Knowledge Quiz.

Again, no frills here, just a test of your general darts knowledge ...

1. What have Jim Bowen, Freddie Flintoff and Dave Spikey got in common?
2. Can you win a game of 501 with a bullseye?
3. True or false – Stephen Fry is a huge darts fan?
4. What country is the 2019 and 2020 Women's World Champion Mikuru Suzuki from?
5. The numbers 159, 162, 163, 165, 166, 168 and 169 are all what?
6. According to research what percentage of accuracy does the average professional darts player throw a dart at the intended target?
    a. 40%
    b. 50%
    c. 60%.
7. What honour was Eric Bristow awarded in 1989?
    a. A Knighthood
    b. MBE
    c. Freedom of the City of London.
8. What was Michael van Gerwen's first major PDC tournament win?
9. Who won the first edition of the World Matchplay in 1994?
10. Who was the commentator for Paul Lim's nine-dart finish in 1990?
    a. Sid Waddell
    b. John Gwynne
    c. Tony Green.

Quiz 76

Legends Quiz: Jocky Wilson.

One of the biggest names of all time in darts – a genuine legend of the game – and here's ten questions for you to figure out ...

1. Which year did Jocky turn pro?
    a. 1978
    b. 1979
    c. 1980.
2. How many times was Jocky crowned as World Champion?
3. True or false – Jocky decided not to become a founder member of the PDC?
4. Jocky spent much of his younger years where?
    a. Overseas
    b. In an orphanage
    c. In a boarding school.
5. Which armed force did Jocky serve in between 1966 and 1968?
6. Jocky was a popular guest on which ITV show?
7. True or false – Jocky was once the subject of a Dexys Midnight Runners hit?
8. Where was Jocky's wife Malvina born?
    a. Brazil
    b. Argentina
    c. Cuba.
9. Did Jocky once work as a coalman or a fish processor – or both?
10. Which nation did Jocky represent?

Quiz 77

The Luke Littler Quiz.

He's the biggest thing to happen in PDC darts – maybe ever. Here are ten questions on Luke Littler ...

1. Where was Luke Littler born – Runcorn or St Helens?
2. What age did Luke begin playing toy darts?
    a. 18 months
    b. 24 months
    c. 36 months.
3. Luke scored his first 180 aged – 5, 6 or 7?
4. How old was Luke when he recorded his first nine-dart finish?
    a. 13
    b. 14
    c. 15.
5. In his debut PDC World Championship, Luke's average was the highest ever for a first-time player. Was it 104.7 or 106.12?
6. What brand of darts does Luke use?
7. What part-time job does Luke's dad do?
8. After the 2024 PDC World Championship, Luke's Instagram increased from 4,000 followers to how many?
    a. 100,000
    b. 500,000
    c. 1.5m.
9. Name two of the opponents Luke faced when he achieved his first three televised nine-dart finishes?
10. Who is Luke's favourite Rugby League side?

Quiz 78

The Random Bunch Quiz.

Here's an eclectic ten questions about anything and everything ...

1. What is unique about the format used for the World Grand Prix tournament?
2. Can you name the one way you can check out 156 in three darts?
3. Tricky one! The thickness of a dart's flight is measured in what unit?
4. Can you name three of the four individual components that make up a standard dart?
5. If a player starts a leg of 501 with seven treble 20s, one treble 19 and one double 12, what have they hit?
6. Which venue was the 2025 PDC World Grand Prix held at?
7. Where was the first World Series of Darts event held in 2013?
    a. Bahrain
    b. Dubai.
8. Which classic Beatles track did Chris Dobey once walk on to?
9. While we're on Dobey, how did he earn his 'Hollywood' nickname?
10. Who's nickname was 'The Project'?
    a. Jan van der Rassel
    b. Jason Lovett.

Quiz 79

The Luke Humphries Quiz.

Another huge star of PDC darts – the one and only Luke Humphries. Can you answer these ten?

1. Who did Luke Humphries beat in the 2024 World Championship final?
2. Where does his nickname 'Cool Hand Luke' come from – a movie or a song?
3. Where was Humphries born – Crewe or Newbury?
4. Who did Luke partner in the 2024 World Cup of Darts?
5. True or false – Luke's father named him as an acronym for Leeds United Kings of Europe?
6. What job did Luke have prior to becoming a full-time darts pro?
7. In 2021 Luke decided to lose weight to help his career. How much did he lose?
    a. 2 stone
    b. 3 stone
    c. 4 stone.
8. Which year was Luke born?
    a. 1992
    b. 1995
    c. 1997.
9. Who beat Luke in the 2021 UK Open – his first major televised final?
10. What was Luke's previous walk-on music to 'I Predict A Riot'?

Quiz 80

Legends Quiz: Bobby George.

With more bling than a king, here is a quiz on the legend that is Bobby George ...

1. What age did Bobby take up darts?
    a. 15
    b. 25
    c. 30.
2. How many times was Bobby a World Championship runner-up?
3. Which Run DMC song did Bobby perform on in 2010 for Sport Relief?
4. The 'King of Bling' was also known as what?
5. Where was Bobby born?
6. Which previous job did Bobby do? Bouncer or taxi driver?
7. True or false – darts player Richie George is Bobby's son?
8. Which hobby is Bobby keen on – snooker or fishing?
9. True or false – Bobby's real name is Charlie Bristow?
10. Name the Queen anthem Bobby walks on to?

Quiz 81

Yep, Another Nicknames Quiz.

This is the gift that keeps giving – you know the drill by now ...

1. Who is known as the 'Mad Monk'?
2. Who called himself 'Champagne'?
3. Which old TV kids character did Ben Hazel call himself?
4. Brian Derbyshire kept things simple with his nickname. What was it?
5. Brian Raman's nickname sounds like he needs to avoid heavy lifting!?
6. Brian Woods's nickname has bird-like qualities – any guesses?
7. Boris Koltsov's Nordic warrior nickname was what?
8. Clive Barden's nickname sounds like a fairground snack. Can you name it?
9. Who had the nickname 'Fingers'?
10. Colin Lloyd went for a great white shark movie title for his nickname. Can you guess it?

Quiz 82

Legends Quiz: Raymond van Barneveld.

Yep, we've hit a rich vein of legends quizzes – and imagine if there wasn't one on Raymond van Barneveld? Well, there is!

1. Where was Barney born? Amsterdam or The Hague?
2. How many PDC World Championships has he won?
3. Is he right-handed or left-handed?
4. Which song does Barney walk on to?
5. How many times has Barney won the World Cup of Darts?
6. After a 7-1 Premier League defeat in March 2019, Barney announced he was retiring. Who beat him?
7. How many televised nine-dart finishes has he achieved as of June 2025?
8. Which Dutch football team does Barney follow? Feyenoord or Den Haag?
9. True or false – in 2017, Van Barneveld featured in the song '180 Linkerbaan' (180 left lane) by Dutch rapper Donnie?
10. In 2006, Barney received which award?
    a. PDC Best Newcomer
    b. PDC Young Player of the Year.

Quiz 83

More Nicknames Quiz.

Let's face it, walk-on music and nicknames **IS** darts – so keep 'em coming we say!

1. Who is known as the Singapore Slinger?
2. Who is known as 'The Rebel'?
3. Do you know Jerry Hendriks's nickname?
4. Keith Deller's nickname rhymed with his surname. What was it?
5. Kim Huybrechts shares his nickname with snooker player Alex Higgins. What is it?
6. Josh Rock is simply known as what?
7. Martin Schindler took his nickname from a similar sounding Steven Spielberg movie?
8. England's Paul Hogan took his nickname from his Australian namesake's most famous character. What was it?
9. Richie Burnett's royal nickname was once shared by King Charles. What is it?
10. Who is known as 'Rapid'?

Quiz 84

Legends Quiz: Phil Taylor.

Yep, we saved the greatest of them all until quiz 84. Let's get going on darts GOAT – Phil Taylor ...

1. How many world titles did Phil Taylor win?
    a. 16
    b. 14
    c. 12.
2. How many World Championship finals (PDC and BDO) did Taylor contend?
    a. 17
    b. 19
    c. 21.
3. How many World Championship match wins did Taylor achieve?
    a. 100
    b. 105
    c. 110.
4. What is Taylor's longest unbeaten run at the World Darts Championship?
    a. 35
    b. 44
    c. 50.
5. How many World Championships did Taylor compete in?
    a. 20
    b. 23
    c. 25.
6. Taylor became the oldest PDC World Champion yet in 2013. How old was he?
    a. 9
    b. 51
    c. 52.

Phil 'The Power' Taylor

7. In 2009 Taylor won every televised ranking event. How many was that?
    a. 5
    b. 7
    c. 9.
8. What was Taylor's walk-on music?
9. True or false – you are more likely to find Taylor at the Britannia Stadium than Vale Park when watching football?
10. Before he adopted 'The Power' nickname, Taylor was known as what?

Quiz 85

The 'A Bit More Bully' Quiz.

Yep, even more trivia on the greatest TV darts show ever.

1. What was the first round questions board known as?
2. Which of these was not a regular category?
    a. Cartoons
    b. Current Affairs
    c. Words.
3. How many sections was the category board split into?
    a. 8
    b. 10
    c. 12.
4. How many questions did each contestant get?
5. How was the value of a correct question worked out?
6. How much was every point worth in the 'Pounds for Points' round?
7. How many bendy Bullys were handed out on each show?
    a. 2
    b. 4
    c. 6.
8. What did the professional player who scored the most points for charity win at the end of each series?
9. On Bully's Prize Board, what could you win if you hit the bullseye?
10. If you hit the bullseye during a 'Pounds for Points' round what would you win?
    a. A prize
    b. No prizes
    c. Score 50 points.

Quiz 86

The Knowledge Quiz – Part 1.

Calling all darts aficionados – here's a technical quiz that you can boast about (so long as you get them all right!) ...

1. What is the body of a dart called?
2. What is the connecting piece between the barrel and the flight called?
3. What are the colourful, four-piece ends of a dart called?
4. What is the typical tungsten composition of a professional dart?
    a. 50%+
    b. 65%+
    c. 80%+.
5. What is the official name of a PDC dartboard?
    a. Pig Board
    b. Bristle Board.
6. During a game, the referee is also known as:
    a. The Scorer
    b. The Caller
    c. The Adder.
7. What are the thin wires of a dartboard also known as?
8. How many points is a 'Baby Fish' worth?
9. To hit a 'basement' shot is to score what?
10. Hitting a treble 20, treble five and treble one is known as a what?

Quiz 87

Obscure Nicknames Quiz.

If you get these ten fairly obscure nicknames, take a bow ... either that or you have sneaked a peak at the answers page!

1. The 'Lethal Biscuit' was once the nickname of who?
    a. James Wilson
    b. Jamie Bain.
2. Jason Clark was known as what?
    a. Cockney Jock
    b. The Scottish Joe.
3. Which Marvel hero did Jim Widmayer take his nickname from?
4. Jeffery de Zwaan was known as what?
    a. The Black Cobra
    b. The Blackbird.
5. John O'Shea chose a name of one of Batman's nemeses. Which one?
6. John MaGowan's nickname suggests he was short-sighted – was it 'Mr Magoo' or 'Specsavers John'?
7. Who was the 'Dutch Dragon'?
8. Justin Hood elected not to go with 'Robin' as his nickname and chose an animated film title about penguins instead. What is it?
9. Who is known as 'The Needle'?
10. Ken McNeill was known as what?
    a. Silver Darts
    b. Golden Darts
    c. Bronze Darts.

Quiz 88

The Knowledge Quiz – Part 2.

This part is more about scoring – a maths test of sorts!

1. What is the highest possible checkout in darts?
2. True or false – You can't checkout on any of these scores: 169, 168, 166, 165, 163, 162 and 159?
3. What are the above seven scores also known as?
4. Officially, what's the highest double on a dartboard?
5. How much is a double top worth?
6. If a player goes 'bust', what does that mean?
7. True or false – if a player goes 'bust', they can choose one scoring dart from their throw?
8. In a PDC contest, what score does each leg begin with?
9. What is a 'whitewash'?
10. True or false – A 'cover shot' is the next best score available if the intended target is blocked?

Quiz 89

The Darts Slang Quiz.

Random descriptions that defy logic – how many do you actually know?

1. What is a score of 76 known as?
    a. Trombone
    b. Trumpet
    c. Tuba.
2. What is each specific segment of a dartboard called?
3. A single 20, five and one is known as a what?
4. What is a 'bail out'?
    a. Hitting a treble with your final dart after hitting two singles?
    b. Hitting 25 three successive times?
5. What is the lower half of a dartboard called?
6. What is a 'hat-trick' in a darts leg?
7. What is a dart that ricochets off the board?
8. When would a game of 'Killer' be used?
9. What are three single ones in one throw called?
10. Hitting a single five with three darts is known as what?

Quiz 90

Michael Smith Quiz.

One of the PDCs most popular players, here's a quick ten on the mighty Michael Smith ...

1. True or false – Smith hit a nine-darter in the 2023 World Championship?
2. How many major finals did Smith lose before winning the 2022 Grand Slam title?
    a. 6
    b. 7
    c. 8.
3. Who was Smith's partner when winning the 2024 World Cup of Darts?
4. What is the title of Smith's walk-on music?
5. Where was he born – Newcastle or St Helens?
6. True or false – Smith's first love was rugby, until he broke his leg aged 15?
7. Who did Smith beat in the 2023 World Championship final?
8. Who did Smith say this of in 2024, "He just tried to think about putting me off, I guess, but lessons learned. I learned my lesson, and he's learned his as well."
    a. Peter Wright
    b. Madars Razma.
9. Does Smith's nickname of 'Bully Boy' stem from a job he had on a farm or his love of the TV show *Bullseye*?
10. True or false – despite hailing from St Helens, Smith supports Warrington Wolves rugby league side?

Quiz 91

The Bits and Bobs Quiz.

No specific topic here – just a bunch of, er, darts-related questions ...

1. Who holds the record for finishing a game in the fastest time of one minute 41 seconds?
2. Who said, "The more games that I did win, the more popular I got, the more followers I got on social media and since then it's not stopped. It's been crazy."
3. What is the diameter of the world's largest dartboard?
    a. 9.6 metres
    b. 10 metres.
4. Who represented England at the 2025 World Cup of Darts?
5. Who said, "It felt hard work and everything you dedicate yourself for, it makes it worthwhile when you achieve things like this."
6. True or false – actor, Steve Coogan was once a professional darts player?
7. What did Women's world number one Beau Greaves achieve at the 2025 UK Open?
8. Who won the 2024 World Seniors Darts Championship?
    a. Phil Taylor
    b. John Henderson.
9. Who won the 2025 World Seniors Darts Championship?
    a. Ross Montgomery
    b. Chris Mason.
10. Where were the above two finals held?
    a. Ally Pally
    b. Marshall Arena
    c. Circus Tavern.

Quiz 92

The Guess What – More Nicknames Quiz.

You know the drill – either figure out who the nickname belongs to or work out the nickname of a named player ...

1. Who is 'The Wizard'?
2. Who is known as the 'Neon Nightmare'?
3. Kevin Doets is known as what?
4. Which Japanese player is known as 'HAL'?
5. Jermaine Wattimena is known as which powerful weapon?
6. Keane Barry is known as what?
7. Who is known as 'The Giant' or simply 'GVV'?
8. Darren Penhall takes the title of a Sade classic song as his nickname. What is it?
9. Who is known as 'The French Touch'?
10. True or false – Dutch player Gian van Veen was actually born in Scotland?

Quiz 93

The Nationalities Quiz – Part 1.

How good are you on our overseas PDC players? You know their names, but do you know where they come from? Let's find out!

1. Where is Madars Razma from?
2. Where is Stowe Buntz from?
3. Is Simon Whitlock from New Zealand or Australia?
4. Where does Haruki Muramatsu hail from?
5. Is Keane Barry from Ireland or Scotland?
6. Which Canadian darts player shares the same name as a former Conservative Prime Minister?
7. Where does Lourence Ilagan come from?
8. Florian Hempel is from:
    a. Belgium
    b. Germany
    c. Latvia.
9. Darren Penhall represents Australia, but what is the country of his birth?
10. True or false – Jermaine Wattimena is from Belgium?

Quiz 94

The Nationalities Quiz – Part 2.

As with Quiz 93, figure out where these ten come from ...

1. Thibault Tricole is from where?
2. Where does Mike Bonser come from?
3. Mickey Mansell – can you name his country of birth?
4. Is Wessel Nijman Dutch or Austrian?
5. Matt Campbell hails from the same nation as John Part. Where is that?
6. Dylan Slevin comes from where?
    a. Northern Ireland
    b. Republic of Ireland.
7. Damon Heta comes from which nation?
8. Is Danny Noppert Belgian or Dutch?
9. True or false – Robert Owen is English?
10. Jeffrey de Graaf is Dutch, Finnish or Swedish?

Quiz 95

Legends Quiz: Fallon Sherrock.

Women's darts is on the rise – and leading the way is the wonderful Fallon Sherrock – here's ten questions on the Queen of the Palace ...

1. Where was Fallon born?
    a. Manchester
    b. Milton Keynes.
2. As of June 2025, how many televised nine-dart finishes had Fallon achieved?
3. Is she right or left-handed?
4. What is Fallon's walk-on music?
5. When did Fallon join the PDC?
    a. 2018
    b. 2019.
6. True or false – in 2011, Fallon won the WDF Girls World Cup?
7. Which year did Fallon receive the MBE?
8. What is Fallon's twin sister – also a darts player – called?
9. As of June 2025, what was Fallon's best performance at the PDC World Championship?
    a. Third round
    b. Fourth round
    c. Fifth round.
10. Who did Fallon beat in the second round of the 2019 PDC World Championship?

Quiz 96

The 'No Way You're Getting Any of These Right' Quiz.

This is all about walk-on music (again) but some are fairly obscure, and others have changed their music – so you're gonna have your work cut out for you!

1. Who used, 'Reach Up (Papa's Got a Brand New Pigbag)' by Perfecto Allstarz?
2. 'Boom, Boom, Boom' by The Outhere Brothers was the music this martial arts-sounding darts star once used. Who is it?
3. 'U Can't Touch This' by MC Hammer was whose walk-on music?
4. Andy Jenkins used a Van Halen classic for his intro. What was it?
5. 'Don't Stop Me Now' by Queen was the music of who?
    a. Ronnie Baxter
    b. Gary Anderson.
6. 'Toxic' by Britney Spears.. who used that as a walk-on?
    a. Anastasia Dobromyslova
    b. Michael Smith.
7. True or false – Beau Greaves used 'Chasing Highs' by Alma?
8. 'Rhinestone Cowboy' by Glen Campbell was Bob Anderson's intro theme – or was it? Yes or No?
9. Callan Rydz uses which Sam Fender song to walk out to?
10. Wham's 'I'm Your Man'– is that Callum Matthews' walk-on song or Keith Deller's?

Quiz 97

The Belgian Waffle Quiz.

All about the many talented Belgian darts stars that have proved so popular in recent times...

1. Who hit a nine-dart finish in the 2025 PDC World Masters?
2. Who is known as 'The Hurricane'?
3. Who is 'The Real Deal'?
4. True or false – One of Dimitri Van den Bergh's middle names is Barbera?
5. What Bruno Mars vocal does Kenny Neyens walk out to?
6. Who walks on to 'Three Little Birds' by Bob Marley?
7. This Belgian star made it to the 2023 World Championship semi-finals, but who is he?
8. Who is known as 'The Believer'?
9. Geert De Vos is known as what?
10. Who represented Belgium at the 2025 World Cup of Darts?

Quiz 98

WDF Legend Quiz: Martin Adams.

We steer off our well-trodden PDC course for a deserved look at a darts legend in anybody's eyes ... Martin Adams

1. What is Martin's nickname?
2. What is his walk-on music?
3. How many World Darts Federation championships has Adams won?
4. In 2001 he achieved his best PDC event placing in the World Matchplay. Was it:
    a. Winner
    b. Runner-up
    c. Semi-finalist.
5. His best highest average was achieved in 2007. What was it?
    a. 110.52
    b. 111
    c. 111.08.
6. Adams was England darts captain for a record period. How long was it?
    a. 10 years
    b. 15 years
    c. 20 years.
7. Where did he work before being made redundant?
    a. Bakery
    b. Brewery
    c. Bank.
8. Is he left or right-handed?
9. True or false – he has never met Phil Taylor competitively?
10. Is this statement correct – Adams has won the British Darts Pentathlon a record 13 times?

Quiz 99

The Another Dose of the True or False Quiz.

The statements below are either true or false (as of 1 June 2025) – just answer one or the other...

1. Luke Humphries has never achieved a televised nine-darter?
2. Michael van Gerwen has won 66 televised events?
3. Stephen Bunting has made six televised nine-dart finishes?
4. In 2020, Jonny Clayton partnered Gerwyn Price to World Cup glory?
5. Chris Dobey won four Players Championship titles in 2024?
6. Nathan Aspinall is a Manchester City supporter?
7. Dave Chisnall was a qualified Vet before turning to darts?
8. Luke Littler hit three nine-dart finishes in 2024?
9. The 2022 World Championship runner-up, Michael Smith, struggled with maths at school, which affected his confidence?
10. James Wade was once in a band called The Mechanics?

Quiz 100

The And Finally Quiz ...

The last ten questions – by this point you should be a walking book of knowledge on darts, so here's one more blast – all centred around the 2025 World Cup of Darts, to round us off ...

1. Who won the 2025 World Cup of Darts?
2. Who were the pair that won the above tournament?
3. Can you name the popular female *Sky Sports* darts presenter?
4. Which two English darts stars named the above presenter as their darts legend in a World Cup Q&A feature?
5. Which nation were the beaten finalists?
6. Who were the beaten finalists' pair?
7. How much did the winning pair win?
    a. £50,000
    b. £80,000.
8. Who started the tournament as top seeds?
9. Which low-ranked nation knocked out Belgium in the group stages?
10. Hosts Germany crashed out at the semi-final stage after losing to Northern Ireland. What score were they beaten by?
    a. 8-1
    b. 8-2
    c. 8-3.

Answers

Quiz 1: The Easing-You-In Points Quiz.
1. 180.
2. 40.
3. 50.
4. Outer bullseye.
5. Six.
6. 5 and 1.
7. b – Shanghai.
8. 45.
9. b – 12.7mm.
10. A double of any number.

Quiz 2: Scores on the Doors Quiz.
1. 3.
2. 120 (Single, double and treble 20).
3. 150.
4. False – unless you need to score 150.
5. 75.
6. 9 (3 x treble 1).
7. 177 – 2 x treble 20, 1 x treble 19.
8. Yes, if they all miss the scoring sections on the board!
9. By going bust which is scoring more than your remaining total.
10. 57 – 3 x treble 19.

Quiz 3: Legends Quiz: Adrian Lewis.

1. Two – 2011, 2012.
2. True, Stoke-on-Trent.
3. 2014.
4. a – Keith Deller.
5. Phil Taylor.
6. Chas & Dave.
7. True – Stoke City (Lewis) and Port Vale (Taylor)
8. Quarter-final.
9. Gary Anderson.
10. 'Jackpot'.

Quiz 4: The 'It's on Random' Quiz.

1. Jocky Wilson.
2. 7-3.
3. Trina Gulliver.
4. USA.
5. Paddy Power.
6. Shaun of the Dead.
7. False.
8. b – £2.5m.
9. £500,000.
10. Nine-dart finishes.

Quiz 5 – The Numbers and Colours Quiz

1. Red.
2. Green.
3. Black.
4. Red and Green.
5. Red and Green.
6. Black.
7. 18 inches.
8. a – 5 feet 8 inches
9. c – 7 feet 9.25 inches.
10. 3,944

Quiz 6: The We Are Premier League Quiz!

1. 8.
2. 6.
3. Triple Crown.
4. b – 44.
5. c – 7.
6. a – £1m.
7. True.
8. O2 Arena.
9. 5.
10. Luke Littler.

Quiz 7: Legends of the Game Quiz

1. 1995.
2. Dennis Priestley.
3. John Part – 2003 & 2008.
4. 14.
5. 18.
6. 3.
7. 4.
8. Gerwyn Price.
9. They all defended their title successfully at least once.
10. They were both called Luke.

Quiz 8: The Nicknames Quiz.

1. Peter Wright.
2. Luke Littler.
3. Alan Norris.
4. Gary Anderson.
5. Luke Humphries.
6. Michael van Gerwen.
7. Jonny Clayton.
8. Gerwyn Price.
9. Nathan Aspinall.
10. Stephen Bunting.

Quiz 9: The PDC World Matchplay Quiz (as of June 2025).

1. 1994.
2. Empress Ballroom, Winter Gardens, Blackpool.
3. Marshall Arena, Milton Keynes.
4. 2020.
5. Dennis Priestley.
6. American.
7. True.
8. James Wade.
9. a – Rod Harrington 2 (Rob Cross 1).
10. c – 24.

Quiz 10: The Know Your Clockface Quiz.

1. 20 and 6.
2. 19 and 17.
3. True.
4. 1 and 4.
5. 39.
6. Winmau.
7. 5 and 1.
8. 108.
9. 11 and 9.
10. 52 – 2x20, 2x5 and 2x1.

Quiz 11: Legends Quiz: James Wade.

1. 4.
2. 3.
3. World number two.
4. Left-handed.
5. c – 13.
6. Helen Chamberlain.
7. a – Chas Hodges.
8. True.
9. b – Winter Gardens, Blackpool.
10. a – Surrey.

Quiz 12: Oh, Referee! The Russ Bray Quiz.

1. a – 28 years.
2. 'The Voice'.
3. False – he was a police traffic officer.
4. Phil Taylor.
5. Eric Bristow.
6. Hitting the bullseye from ten feet.
7. Luke Littler and Luke Humphries.
8. a – PDC Ambassador.
9. c – West Ham.
10. a – Boxing.

Quiz 13: The Darts General Trivia Quiz.

1. c – 2005.
2. True.
3. 50 grams.
4. Peter Wright.
5. a – Amazing Greys.
6. b – 4.8m.
7. False.
8. c – His Wife.
9. c – 82.
10. Leyton Orient.

Quiz 14: Legends Quiz: Michael van Gerwen.

1. 3.
2. 7.
3. Football.
4. False.
5. a – Tiler.
6. b – Mighty Mike.
7. True.
8. a – PSV.
9. 10.
10. Yes.

Quiz 15: The Bristow or Mason Quiz.

1. Eric Bristow.
2. Chris Mason.
3. Chris Mason.
4. Eric Bristow.
5. Chris Mason.
6. Eric Bristow.
7. Eric Bristow.
8. Chris Mason.
9. Eric Bristow.
10. Chris Mason.

The Darts Pioneers Quiz – Part 1.

1. c – 1973-1977.
2. Fred Truman.
3. True.
4. Bar Billiards, Pool, Arm Wrestling, Table Skittles, Table Football & Shove Ha'Penny were all featured.
5. a – By saying "I'll Si'Thee".
6. b – Doubles board.
7. True.
8. a – 62.
9. b – The second series.
10. a – Colin Minton.

Quiz 17: The One and Only – It's the Sid Waddell Quiz.

1. Cliff Lazarenko.
2. Keith Deller.
3. Phil Taylor.
4. Phil Taylor.
5. Jocky Wilson.
6. Eric Bristow.
7. Steve Beaton.
8. Phil Taylor.
9. John Lowe.
10. Phil Taylor.

Quiz 18: Whose Favourite Doubles Quiz

1. 14.
2. 12.
3. 18.
4. 16.
5. 20.
6. 16.
7. 4.
8. 16.
9. 10.
10. 16.

Quiz 19: It's the Darts Cricket Quiz.

1. True.
2. Mickey Mouse.
3. Hit it three times.
4. Hit the treble of that number.
5. Yes.
6. Nearest the bullseye.
7. False.
8. 3.
9. Soft tip.
10. False.

Quiz 20: The Walk-on Music Quiz – Part 1.

1. Florian Hempel.
2. 'Crazy Crazy Nights'.
3. Ryan Meikle.
4. Mensur Suljović.
5. 'Song 2'.
6. 'Hooked on a Feeling' by Blue Swede.
7. Robert Owen.
8. Jim Williams.
9. 'T.N.T.'.
10. 'Welcome to the Jungle' by Guns N' Roses.

Quiz 21: The Know Your History Quiz!

1. b – 1908.
2. Arrows.
3. Turkey feathers.
4. c – Wood.
5. c – France.
6. A quadruple scoring ring to achieve a maximum of 240 for three darts.
7. c `– Tennis.
8. A double.
9. c – 1.
10. a – 1973.

Quiz 22: The This and That Quiz.

1. Gerwyn Price.
2. Peter Wright.
3. 301.
4. The Manchester Dartboard.
5. Eric Bristow.
6. The PDC Qualifying School where players can win a two-year PDC Tour Card.
7. Hawaii Five-O.
8. 'The Dragon'.
9. Russ Bray.
10. 'Don't Look Back in Anger'.

Quiz 23: The Nine-darters Quiz.

1. c – 2002.
2. Paul Lim.
3. b – 12.
4. 11.
5. James Wade.
6. Michael van Gerwen.
7. Michael van Gerwen.
8. 3.
9. 1.
10. True – 4.

Quiz 24: The Walk-On Music Quiz – Part 2.

1. Nathan Aspinall.
2. Luke Humphries.
3. Gary Anderson.
4. Raymond van Barneveld.
5. Stephen Bunting.
6. Peter Wright.
7. 'Greenlight' by Pitbull.
8. 'Let's Get Ready to Rumble'.
9. 'Shut Up and Dance' by Walk the Moon.
10. 'Johnny B. Goode' by Chuck Berry.

Quiz 25: The PDC Hall of Fame Quiz.

1. 2015.
2. John Lowe and Eric Bristow.
3. c – 2008.
4. John Part (2017).
5. b – John Gwynne.
6. Russ Bray.
7. Barry Hearn.
8. Phil Taylor.
9. Referee.
10. Dennis Priestley.

Quiz 26: The Brainteaser Quiz.

1. Numbers 1-20 can all be scored with 1 dart, treble 7 is 21 and double 11 is 22. More than 1 dart is needed with top score of 23.
2. a – Chicago.
3. Netherlands.
4. Bahrain Masters.
5. Raymond van Barneveld.
6. Darren Webster.
7. Dimitri Van den Bergh.
8. Rob Cross.
9. Steve Beaton.
10. Ear defenders!

Quiz 27: The Guess Who Quiz.

1. Peter Wright ('Snakebite').
2. Adrian Lewis ('Jackpot').
3. Luke Littler.
4. Raymond van Barneveld.
5. Michael van Gerwen.
6. 'Big Cliff' (Cliff Lazarenko).
7. Rob Cross (Voltage).
8. 'Bully Boy' (Michael Smith).
9. Robbie Green ('Kong').
10. 'Double Dekker' (Jan Dekker).

Quiz 28: The Scores on the Doors Quiz.

1. a – 11-7.
2. Richie Burnett.
3. Gerwyn Price.
4. 4.
5. True.
6. 3.
7. 3, between 2015-2017
8. 7-4.
9. Yes – 2020, 2023 and 2025.
10. Peter Manley.

Quiz 29: Legends Quiz: Dennis Priestley.

1. True.
2. 'The Menace'.
3. 'Hell Raiser' by The Sweet.
4. Eric Bristow.
5. a – Newsagent.
6. Coal merchant.
7. 1.
8. World Matchplay.
9. Phil Taylor.
10. a – Barnsley.

Quiz 30: The TV Arrows Quiz.

1. *Indoor League*.
2. True.
3. Game of Throws.
4. Piccadilly Radio.
5. b – Oldham Athletic.
6. c – 2004.
7. True.
8. b – 2.
9. *Coronation Street*.
10. *Phoenix Nights*.

Quiz 31: True or false Eric Bristow Quiz.
1. False – it was Hackney.
2. True.
3. True.
4. True.
5. False.
6. True.
7. True.
8. False.
9. True.
10. False – he finished fourth in 2012.

Quiz 32: Jobs for the Boys.
1. Barman.
2. Postman.
3. Car mechanic.
4. Accountant.
5. Coalminer.
6. Carpenter.
7. Schoolboy.
8. Rugby League player.
9. Tyre fitter.
10. Plasterer.

Quiz 33: The World Cup of Darts Quiz – Part 1.

1. 40.
2. 2.
3. 2010.
4. a – Raymond van Barneveld and Co Stompé.
5. 5.
6. Phil Taylor and Adrian Lewis.
7. Germany.
8. England.
9. False – Smith has one title.
10. b – Frankfurt (seven).

Quiz 34: Record Breakers.

1. Michael van Gerwen achieved this incredible three-dart average in the 2016 Premier League match against Michael Smith.
2. Nine-dart finish.
3. Gary Anderson.
4. Phil Taylor.
5. Phil Taylor.
6. World Champion.
7. Luke Littler (17).
8. 45.
9. Adrian Lewis (2011).
10. a – 107.60

Quiz 35: The (Even More) Nicknames Quiz.
1. Rob Cross.
2. 'Superchin'.
3. Gabriel Clemens.
4. Michael Smith.
5. James Wade.
6. Fallon Sherrock.
7. Adrian Lewis.
8. 'The Heat'.
9. Chris Dobey.
10. 'Chizzy'.

Quiz 36: The More About Sid Waddell Quiz.
1. Newcastle United.
2. 'The Voice of Darts'.
3. a – Alnwick.
4. 'The Thief of Bad Gags'.
5. c – 1994.
6. True, for a documentary he made in a series called *Ipso Facto*.
7. Sloggers.
8. False – it was banned, but in 1973.
9. 2013.
10. Elvis Presley.

Quiz 37: Who Said That?

1. a – Eric Bristow.
2. a – Eric Bristow.
3. a – Sid Waddell.
4. b – Bobby George.
5. a – Andy Fordham.
6. b – Bobby George.
7. a – Sid Waddell.
8. a – Andy Fordham.
9. b – Eric Bristow.
10. a – Peter Wright.

Quiz 38: Legends Quiz: John Part.

1. b – Toronto.
2. 2.
3. True.
4. c – 3.
5. b – 2013.
6. 1.
7. 2.
8. b – Quarter-final.
9. True.
10. b – 'Maple'.

Quiz 39: The World Cup of Darts Quiz – Part 2.

1. Wales.
2. Gerwyn Price and Jonny Clayton.
3. 2010.
4. England (five times).
5. b – 4.
6. b – 4.
7. 2.
8. 5.
9. True.
10. Australia 2022.

Quiz 40: Stand Up if You Love Ally Pally!

1. b – 2008.
2. 2019/20.
3. c – 90,000.
4. a – 'Chase The Sun' by Planet Funk.
5. b – 500,000.
6. a – London.
7. a – 1873.
8. a – 10 miles.
9. c – 3,500.
10. a – Dame Gracie Fields.

Quiz 41: The Darts Pioneers Quiz – Part 2.

1. a – 1927-1997.
2. c – Phil Taylor.
3. True.
4. Yes.
5. Eric Bristow.
6. The Swede became the first foreigner to win the title.
7. False.
8. b – 2.
9. c – 1,000.
10. 2.

Quiz 42: The Before They Were Famous Quiz.

1. a – Butcher.
2. Barber.
3. a – Coffee shop.
4. Handball.
5. Painter & decorator.
6. Electrician.
7. Cattle Worker.
8. a – Plumber.
9. Schoolboy.
10. a – Warehouse.

Quiz 43: The When Darts Goes Wrong Quiz

1. Peter Wright.
2. Gerwyn Price.
3. Gerwyn Price.
4. Gerwyn Price.
5. Daryl Gurney.
6. Peter Manley.
7. a – Adrian Lewis v Gerwyn Price
8. Adrian Lewis.
9. Peter Wright.
10. Paul' Nicholson.

Quiz 44: The Make Mine a Double Quiz.

1. Double 1.
2. Double 3.
3. A checkout that ends with 1, 2 or even three bullseyes.
4. Double 11 (22).
5. Fish, chips and peas.
6. a – Sunset Strip.
7. Umbrellas.
8. A single four and a double top (x 20) in reference to soul group The Four Tops.
9. 88.
10. Varieties – in reference to Heinz 57 Varieties.

Quiz 45: That's Darts Quiz.

1. When a player can't release a dart during a throw through motor skill difficulties.
2. True.
3. When a player is looking to check-out with a double, a marker is often thrown just outside the board near the double required to help guide in the next dart.
4. Leaning as far of the oche when they throw their darts.
5. Hitting a single when aiming for a double.
6. To finish a game with a double, double.
7. To win the game.
8. Popcorn.
9. Between the two ones that make up the 11 numbering on a board.
10. 95.

Quiz 46: Legends Quiz: Keith Deller.

1. 'Milky Bar Kid' and 'Delboy'.
2. b – 1983.
3. Eric Bristow.
4. True.
5. a – Ipswich.
6. Right-handed.
7. True.
8. 'Things Can Only Get Better'.
9. b – 97 seconds.
10. c – MBE.

Quiz 47: The PDC Prize Money Quiz.

1. £500,000
2. c – £1m.
3. a – £350,000.
4. False – £225,000.
5. False – the Grand Slam winner gets £25,000 less.
6. a – £150,000.
7. c – £5m.
8. Less – £150,000.
9. UK Open.
10. True.

Quiz 48: Location, Location.

1. Warrington.
2. Crewe.
3. a – James Wade.
4. St Helens.
5. a – Rob Cross.
6. Gerwyn Price.
7. Jonny Clayton.
8. False – Livingstone.
9. Phil Taylor.
10. b – Stockport.

Quiz 49: Darts Players and Football – Part 1.
1. James Maddison.
2. b – Manchester City.
3. Manchester United.
4. Leeds United.
5. Manchester United.
6. Hibernian.
7. Newcastle United.
8. Stoke City.
9. PSV Eindhoven.
10. b – Liverpool.

Quiz 50: Darts Players and Football – Part 2.
1. Liverpool.
2. Den Haag.
3. Tottenham.
4. Port Vale.
5. Manchester United.
6. No – Liverpool.
7. Chelsea.
8. Norwich City.
9. Manchester United.
10. a – Royal Antwerp.

Quiz 51: The History Makers.
1. Ted Evetts.
2. Rob Cross.
3. Brendan Dolan.
4. a – 914.
5. Michael Smith.
6. c – 24.
7. c – 42 (Anderson 22-20 MVG).
8. Luke Littler.
9. John Part, Canada.
10. Raymond van Barneveld and Michael van Gerwen.

Quiz 52: Legends quiz: Rob Cross.
1. 'I Don't Wanna Wait' by David Guetta and OneRepublic.
2. Right-handed.
3. 2019.
4. 2019.
5. b – 2.
6. 7.
7. Phil Taylor.
8. a – Michael Smith.
9. a – 1.
10. Michael van Gerwen.

Quiz 53: The Stephen Bunting Quiz.
1. 'Let's go Bunting mental!'
2. 'Surfin' Bird' by Trashmen.
3. St Helens.
4. Peter Griffin.
5. c – TikTok.
6. 2024.
7. 2.
8. 2014.
9. Anfield (Liverpool FC).
10. c – Both a + b.

Quiz 54: Who Said It.
1. Peter Wright.
2. Sid Waddell.
3. Dennis Priestley.
4. Luke Littler.
5. Phil Taylor.
6. Adrian Lewis.
7. Michael van Gerwen.
8. Phil Taylor.
9. Peter Wright.
10. Michael van Gerwen.

Quiz 55: Legends Quiz: John Lowe.

1. 'Here I Go Again' by Whitesnake.
2. True.
3. c – 102,000.
4. a – Old Stoneface.
5. c – 28.
6. a – Sunderland.
7. True.
8. c – Carpenter.
9. False.
10. b – John Lowe.

Quiz 56: The Luke or Luke Quiz.

1. Luke Littler.
2. Luke Humphries.
3. Luke Littler.
4. Luke Humphries.
5. Luke Humphries.
6. Luke Littler.
7. Luke Humphries.
8. Luke Littler.
9. Luke Humphries.
10. Luke Littler.

Quiz 57: The Nine-darters Quiz.

1. James Wade.
2. John Lowe 1984.
3. Paul Lim.
4. Phil Taylor 2010 Premier League final.
5. Adrian Lewis 2011.
6. Michael Smith 2023.
7. Fallon Sherrock.
8. Luke Littler in 2024 aged 16 years and 363 days old.
9. b – the final three darts of the nine.
10. True.

Quiz 58: The General Legends Quiz.

1. Eric Bristow.
2. The Circus Tavern, Purfleet.
3. John Lowe 1970s, 1980s and 1990s.
4. Cliff Lazarenko.
5. Jocky Wilson during their song 'Jackie Wilson Says'.
6. Bobby George.
7. Eric Bristow.
8. 97 seconds.
9. John Part.
10. 15.

Quiz 59: Legends Quiz: Peter Manley.

1. 3.
2. Phil Taylor.
3. 'One Dart'.
4. 'Amarillo' by Tony Christie.
5. 'Who Are You?' by The Who.
6. The Desert Classic in 2003.
7. a – Wayne Mardle.
8. c – 2 years.
9. False.
10. b – 2.

Quiz 60: The More Walk-on Music Quiz.

1. Dimitri Van den Bergh.
2. 'I'm Still Standing' by Elton John.
3. 'Red Light Spells Danger'.
4. 'Paranoid' by Black Sabbath.
5. 'Sweet Caroline' by Neil Diamond.
6. 'Zombie'.
7. Rob Cross.
8. Vic Reeves and 'Dizzy'.
9. Katy Perry.
10. 'Ice Ice Baby' by Vanilla Ice.

Quiz 61: The PDC – How Much Do You Know?

1. Professional Darts Corporation.
2. Eddie Hearn.
3. 1992.
4. PDC World Championship/World Matchplay/Premier League/Grand Slam/UK Open/World Grand Prix.
5. World Darts Council.
6. a – Brentwood.
7. Dennis Priestley.
8. Phil Taylor.
9. £2.5m.
10. b – Anglia TV.

Quiz 62: The Even More Nicknames Quiz – Legends Special.

1. Eric Bristow.
2. Phil Taylor.
3. Raymond van Barneveld.
4. John Lowe.
5. Wayne Mardle.
6. Dennis Priestley.
7. 'The Viking'.
8. 'The Special One'.
9. Jan Dekker.
10. Bobby George.

Quiz 63: Darts Terminology and Slang A-Z – Part 1.

1. Arrows.
2. Bail out.
3. Bed and Breakfast.
4. The big fish.
5. Bullseye.
6. It is a way of deciding who starts the game – the player nearest the bull gets to throw first.
7. Busted.
8. Chalk and blackboard – either or both are correct.
9. A 'Champagne Finish'.
10. Check-Out.

Quiz 64: The Even More Who Said This Quiz.

1. Chris Mason.
2. Chris Mason.
3. Chris Mason.
4. Bobby George.
5. Bobby George.
6. Sid Waddell.
7. Sid Waddell.
8. Ray Stubbs.
9. Mervyn King.
10. Bobby George.

Bobby George

Quiz 65: Darts Terminology and Slang Quiz A-Z – Part 2.

1. When a checkout requires two more darts to win the game – one being a double.
2. 40.
3. 501.
4. 1.
5. 9.
6. The Oche.
7. When a dart lands in the stem of a dart already in the board.
8. A finish that involves the three segments of the same number – single, treble and double.
9. Three darts in the single one bed.
10. Flight.

Quiz: 66: The Greatest Darts Show Ever Quiz?

1. Jim Bowen.
2. Tony Green.
3. Bully.
4. a – 1981.
5. Bully's Prize Board.
6. Nothing for two in a bed.
7. c – 14.
8. Dave Spikey and Andrew 'Freddie' Flintoff.
9. Bus Fare Home.
10. "Look at what you could have won."

Quiz 67: Legends Quiz: Gary Anderson.

1. b – 2.
2. 2015 & 2016.
3. a – 2.
4. b – Builder.
5. True.
6. b – Hibs.
7. 'The Flying Scotsman'.
8. 'Dreamboy'.
9. 3.
10. Jeffrey de Graaf.

Quiz 68: The All-England Quiz.

1. Northumberland.
2. Kent.
3. St Helens.
4. Kent.
5. Somerset.
6. Yorkshire.
7. Newcastle.
8. Norfolk.
9. Newcastle.
10. Worcestershire.

Quiz 69: The We All Love A Bit More Bully Quiz.

1. A bendy Bully toy.
2. c – 6.
3. a – Central.
4. b – Speedboat.
5. 101.
6. a – Peter Williams.
7. True.
8. Sunday.
9. c – 15-20m.
10. 30 minutes.

Quiz 70: Nicknames Quiz (again).

1. 'The Wizard'.
2. Glen Durrant.
3. 'The Dreammaker'.
4. 'The Rockstar'.
5. Stephen Bunting.
6. Adonis.
7. Gabriel Clemens
8. 'Heavy Metal'.
9. 'The Lipstick'.
10. 'Big Cliff'.

Quiz 71: Darts Players and Their Football Teams.

1. Ipswich Town.
2. Nottingham Forest.
3. Manchester United.
4. Ajax.
5. Rangers.
6. West Ham United.
7. Arbroath.
8. Chelsea.
9. Sunderland.
10. Arsenal.

Quiz 72: Random Trivia Quiz.

1. 'Chasing Highs' by Alma.
2. Bob Anderson.
3. True.
4. The oldest World Champion.
5. 'I'm Too Sexy'.
6. Danny Noppert.
7. Eric Bristow or John Part.
8. True.
9. Alex Roy.
10. False.

Quiz 73: The Iconic Venues Quiz.

1. Alexandra Palace.
2. Circus Tavern.
3. Winter Gardens.
4. Lakeside Country Club.
5. O2 Arena.
6. Butlin's Minehead Resort.
7. Marshall Arena.
8. Mattioli Arena.
9. SSE Arena.
10. WV Active Aldersley.

Quiz 74: True or False Quiz.

1. True.
2. False – it was the UK.
3. True.
4. False – 18 inches.
5. True.
6. False – 170.
7. True.
8. False – there is a game called cricket.
9. False – the dart just counts as zero.
10. True.

Quiz 75: General Knowledge Quiz.

1. They presented the TV show *Bullseye*.
2. Yes.
3. True.
4. Japan.
5. The numbers 159, 162, 163, 165, 166, 168 and 169 are all ... bogey numbers – highest numbers that cannot be taken out with a three-dart finish.
6. b – 50%.
7. b – MBE.
8. World Grand Prix.
9. Larry Butler.
10. c – Tony Green.

Quiz 76: Legends Quiz: Jocky Wilson.

1. b – 1979.
2. 2.
3. False – he was a founding member.
4. b – In an orphanage.
5. The Army.
6. *Bullseye*.
7. False – their hit was 'Jackie Wilson Says'.
8. b – Argentina. <Where Malvina was born>
9. Both.
10. 10. Scotland.

Quiz 77: The Luke Littler Quiz.

1. Runcorn.
2. a – 18 months.
3. 6.
4. a – 13.
5. 106.12.
6. Target.
7. Taxi driver.
8. c – 1.5m.
9. Michael van Gerwen, Nathan Aspinall, Luke Humphries.
10. Warrington Wolves.

Quiz 78: The Random Bunch Quiz.

1. You need a double in and a double out.
2. Treble 20, treble 20, double 18.
3. Microns.
4. Point, Barrel, Stem/Shaft, Flight.
5. A nine-dart finish.
6. Mattioli Arena in Leicester.
7. b – Dubai.
8. 'Hey Jude'.
9. By wearing a baseball cap while playing.
10. a – Jan van der Rassel

Luke 'The Nuke' Littler

Quiz 79: The Luke Humphries Quiz.

1. Luke Littler.
2. Movie (same name, 1967).
3. Newbury.
4. Michael Smith.
5. True.
6. Roofer.
7. c – 4 stone.
8. b – 1995.
9. James Wade.
10. 'Cake by the Ocean' by DNCE.

Quiz 80: Legends Quiz: Bobby George.

1. c – 30.
2. 2 times.
3. 'Walk This Way'.
4. 'Bobby Dazzler' or 'Mr Glitter'.
5. London.
6. Bouncer.
7. True.
8. Fishing.
9. False.
10. 'We Are The Champions'.

James Wade

Quiz 81: Yep, Another Nicknames Quiz.
1. Arron Monk.
2. Barrie Bates.
3. *Mr Benn*
4. Derby.
5. Glass Back.
6. Pecker.
7. 'The Viking'.
8. Hotdog.
9. Chris Loudon.
10. Jaws.

Quiz 82: Legends Quiz: Raymond van Barneveld.
1. The Hague.
2. 1 – plus four BDO titles.
3. Right.
4. 'Eye of the Tiger' by Survivor.
5. 4.
6. Michael van Gerwen.
7. 5.
8. Den Haag.
9. True.
10. a – PDC Best Newcomer.

Quiz 83: More Nicknames Quiz.
   1. Paul Lim.
   2. Jeffrey de Graaf.
   3. 'Electric'.
   4. 'The Fella'.
   5. 'The Hurricane'.
   6. 'Rocky'.
   7. 'The List'.
   8. 'Crocodile Dundee'.
   9. 'The Prince of Wales'.
   10. Ricky Evans.

Quiz 84: Legends Quiz: Phil Taylor.
   1. a – 16 (Including his 2 BDO titles).
   2. b – 19.
   3. c – 110.
   4. b – 44.
   5. c – 25.
   6. c – 52.
   7. b – 7.
   8. 'The Power' by Snap!
   9. False, he is more likely to attend Vale Park, home of his team Port Vale.
   10. 'The Crafty Potter'.

Quiz 85: The 'A Bit More Bully' Quiz.

1. The Category Board.
2. a – Cartoons.
3. b – 10.
4. 3.
5. By the points scored on the dartboard by their partner.
6. £1.
7. c – 6.
8. The Bronze Bully.
9. Bully's Special Prize.
10. c – Score 50 points.

Quiz 86: The Knowledge Quiz – Part 1.

1. The barrel.
2. The shaft.
3. Flights.
4. c – 80%+.
5. b – Bristle Board.
6. b – The Caller.
7. Spiders.
8. 130 – 1x treble 20, 1x single 20 and the bullseye.
9. Double 3.
10. 'Champagne breakfast'.

Quiz 87: Obscure Nicknames Quiz.

1. a – James Wilson
2. a – 'Cockney Jock'.
3. 'Captain America'.
4. a – 'The Black Cobra'.
5. 'The Joker'.
6. 'Mr Magoo'.
7. Jules van Dongen.
8. 'Happy Feet'.
9. Keegan Brown.
10. Silver Darts'.

Quiz 88: The Knowledge Quiz – Part 2.

1. 170.
2. True.
3. Bogey numbers.
4. Bullseye.
5. 40 – 2 x 20 points.
6. They have scored more points than they had remaining.
7. False – no dart scores in a bust throw.
8. 501.
9. When one player wins all the legs available (e.g. 5-0).
10. True.

Quiz 89: The Darts Slang Quiz.

1. a – Trombone.
2. Bed.
3. Bed & Breakfast.
4. a) Hitting a treble with the final dart after two single scores
5. Downstairs.
6. Three bullseyes in one throw.
7. A Bounce Out.
8. In training or for a fun game.
9. Lady Lollipop.
10. Garbage Bin.

Quiz 90: Michael Smith Quiz.

1. True.
2. c – 8.
3. Luke Humphries.
4. 'Shut Up and Dance'.
5. St Helens.
6. False – he broke his hip.
7. Michael van Gerwen.
8. b – Madars Razma.
9. It stems from a job he had on a farm.
10. False – he follows St Helens.

Quiz 91: The Bits and Bobs Quiz.
1. Phil Taylor.
2. Luke Littler.
3. a – 9.6 metres.
4. Luke Littler and Luke Humphries.
5. Luke Humphries in 2025.
6. False.
7. She was the first female player to reach the fourth round of the tournament.
8. b – John Henderson.
9. a – Ross Montgomery.
10. c – Circus Tavern.

Quiz 92: The Guess What – More Nicknames Quiz.
1. Simon Whitlock.
2. Stowe Buntz.
3. 'Hawkeye'.
4. Haruki Muramatsu.
5. 'The Machine Gun'.
6. 'Dynamite'.
7. Gian van Veen.
8. 'Smooth Operator'.
9. Thibault Tricole.
10. False.

Quiz 93: The Nationalities Quiz – Part 1.

1. Latvia.
2. Australia.
3. Australia.
4. Japan.
5. Ireland.
6. David Cameron.
7. Philippines.
8. b – Germany.
9. England.
10. False – he is Dutch.

Quiz 94: The Nationalities Quiz – Part 2.

1. France.
2. Australia.
3. Northern Ireland.
4. Dutch.
5. Canada.
6. b – Republic of Ireland.
7. Australia.
8. Dutch.
9. False – he is Welsh.
10. Swedish.

Quiz 95: Legends Quiz: Fallon Sherrock

1. b – Milton Keynes
2. 2.
3. Right.
4. 'Last Friday Night' by Katy Perry.
5. b – 2019.
6. True.
7. 2023.
8. Felicia.
9. a – Third round.
10. Mensur Suljović.

Quiz 96: The 'No Way You're Getting Any of These Right' Quiz.

1. Adrian Lewis.
2. Alan 'Chuck' Norris.
3. Andy Hamilton.
4. Jump.
5. a – Ronnie Baxter.
6. a – Anastasia Dobromyslova.
7. True.
8. Yes.
9. 'Hypersonic Missiles'.
10. Callum Matthews.

Quiz 97: The Belgian Waffle Quiz.

1. Dimitri Van den Bergh.
2. Kim Huybrechts.
3. Mike De Decker.
4. True.
5. 'Uptown Funk'.
6. Mike De Decker.
7. Dimitri Van den Bergh.
8. Kenny Neyens.
9. 'Foxy'. (Geert De Vos' nickname)
10. Mike De Decker and Dimitri Van den Bergh.

Quiz 98: WDF Legend Quiz: Martin Adams.

1. 'Wolfie'.
2. 'Hungry Like the Wolf' by Duran Duran.
3. 3.
4. c – Semi-finalist.
5. a – 110.52.
6. c – 20 years.
7. c – Bank.
8. Right-handed.
9. False.
10. Adams has won the British Darts Pentathlon a record 13 times – correct.

Dimitri Van den Bergh

Quiz 99: The Another Dose of the True or False Quiz.

1. True.
2. True.
3. False – zero so far.
4. True.
5. False – it was 3.
6. False – Manchester United.
7. False.
8. True.
9. True.
10. False.

Quiz 100: The And Finally Quiz ...

1. Northern Ireland.
2. Josh Rock and Daryl Gurney.
3. Emma Paton.
4. Luke Humphries and Luke Littler.
5. Wales.
6. Gerwyn Price and Jonny Clayton.
7. b – £80,000.
8. England.
9. Philippines.
10. a – 8-1.

Emma Paton of Sky Sports during the Cazoo Grand Slam of Darts group match at Aldersley Leisure Village, November 2022 in Wolverhampton